Pillsbury

REAL
HOME
COOKING

Ottenheimer Publishers, Inc.

Publisher: Sally Peters
Publication Manager: Diane B. Anderson
Senior Editor: Elaine Christiansen
Senior Food Editor: Jackie Sheehan
Test Kitchen Coordinator: Pat Peterson
Circulation Specialist: Karen Goodsell
Production Coordinator: Michele Warren
Publication Secretary: Mary Thell
Food Editors: Mary Ellen Berge, Sharon Saldin
Food Stylist: Jo Ann Cherry
Food Stylist's Assistant: Sharon Saldin
Contributing Editor: Patricia Miller
Consulting Editor: William Monn
Home Economists: Pillsbury Publications
Nutrition Information: Pillsbury Technology
Design: Tad Ware & Company, Inc.
Photography: Studio 3

Cover Photo: Apple Apricot Stuffed Pork Chops p. 22

REAL HOME COOKING

A new taste
sensation—
Herb-Marinated
Roast, Page 20

Winter Vegetables
with Rosemary,
Pages 50

It melts in your
mouth—Chocolate
Meringue Dessert,
Page 69

EDITOR'S ⬤Pillsbury NOTEBOOK

REAL HOME COOKING

*Discover or rediscover traditional favorites that
make it worth staying home for dinner.*

The essence of real home cooking hasn't
changed all that much from the days of our
grandmothers, even though our lifestyles are
decidedly different. Busy schedules limit the time
we spend in the kitchen and around the dinner
table, yet we yearn for at-home meals with family
and friends. With recipes in this cookbook, tested
with today's ingredients and cooking styles, you
can achieve home cooked meals just the way you
remember them.

Home Cooking For the 90's
This Classic® Cookbook is a collection of old-
fashioned, but updated favorites. These recipes for
the '90s have:
- Lighter, lower calorie ingredients.
- Easy-to-follow preparations.
- Old-fashioned quality using convenience
  products, make-ahead techniques and microwave
  ovens.
- Recipes for 4 to 6 servings.

"Comfort Food" With a Capital "C"
This month's *Classic Know-How*™ on page
24 features easy-to-follow instructions and step-by-
step photographs for making *Pot Roast and Gravy*—
that all-time family favorite
of meat, potatoes
and vegetables
in one pot.

**For friends or
family—Pot Roast
and Gravy p. 25**

Calling All Waist-watchers

Home cooking is for you, too. We've developed lower-calorie versions of seven favorite main dishes.

These recipes are trimmed of calories but not trimmed of great down-home taste: They are:

- *Cheesy Vegetable Chowder,* 280 calories, page 7.
- *Chicken Cranberry Bake,* 290 calories, page 26.
- *Hamburger Florentine Soup,* 160 calories, page 8.
- *Herbed Buttermilk Stroganoff,* 350 calories, page 10.
- *Lasagna Roll-Ups,* 350 calories, page 19.
- *Salsa Meatloaf,* 290 calories, page 11.
- *Pork and Peppers Stir-Fry,* 190 calories, page 16.

Pictured top to bottom: Winter Green Salad p. 55, Chicken Cranberry Bake p. 26

Home Cooking in Your Kitchen

Real home cooking will never go out of style as long as people enjoy foods with full-bodied flavors. This Classic® Cookbook collection of recipes invites you to prepare traditional recipes with ease that will turn out just as delicious as you remember them.

P.S. For the loves in your life, turn to page 66 for "lovin' from the oven" Valentine surprise ideas!

Make this treat for your sweetheart— Strawberry Cream Puff p. 82

DOWN-HOME MAIN DISHES

Now you can serve delicious dinners and not spend all day making them!

Apple Apricot Stuffed Pork Chops. Cheesy Noodle Casserole. Swiss Steak. Hungarian Goulash. Down-home main dishes like these lie at the heart of American cooking. They're not trendy; they're just tasty. They blend the flavors and foods that have been favorites of families for generations. In our tasty versions, we've trimmed the calories in some, put the microwave to work in others, and pared down ingredients to simplify them all.

Smoked turkey sausage, frozen vegetables and stovetop cooking streamline the preparation in this updated stew.

QUICK SAUSAGE STEW

(pictured on p. 4)

½ lb. smoked turkey sausage, cut into ½-inch slices
½ cup sliced onion
2 teaspoons oil
1 (10½-oz.) can beef consomme
2 cups Green Giant® American Mixtures™ San Francisco Style—Broccoli, Carrots, Water Chestnuts and Red Peppers (from 16-oz. pkg.)
½ teaspoon dried thyme leaves
3 tablespoons cornstarch
3 tablespoons water
  Hot cooked instant rice or couscous

In large skillet over medium-high heat, brown sausage and onion in hot oil. Stir in consomme, frozen vegetables and thyme. Bring to a boil. Reduce heat; cover and simmer 1 to 2 minutes or until vegetables are crisp-tender.

In small bowl, combine cornstarch and water; mix well. Stir into stew. Cook over medium heat until mixture boils and thickens, about 1 minute, stirring constantly. Serve over hot cooked rice or couscous. 3 servings.

NUTRITION INFORMATION PER SERVING

SERVING SIZE: 1/3 OF RECIPE		PERCENT U.S. RDA PER SERVING	
CALORIES	430	PROTEIN	35%
PROTEIN	22 g	VITAMIN A	45%
CARBOHYDRATE	54 g	VITAMIN C	40%
FAT	14 g	THIAMINE	10%
CHOLESTEROL	51 mg	RIBOFLAVIN	6%
SODIUM	1190 mg	NIACIN	15%
POTASSIUM	550 mg	CALCIUM	6%
		IRON	20%

Adding brats to this regional French dish gives it a wonderful flavor. Serve it for friends after your next winter sports activity.

CABBAGE AND BRATWURST

4 slices bacon, cut into 1-inch pieces
2 medium onions, thinly sliced
2 garlic cloves, minced
2 cups thickly sliced carrots
1 medium head (about 2 lb.) cabbage or savoy cabbage, cut into 1-inch chunks
2 whole cloves
1 bay leaf
1 to 1½ lb. cooked bratwurst, cut into 2-inch pieces
1 cup beef broth
½ cup dry white wine, water or beef broth
  Salt and pepper

In 12-inch skillet or Dutch oven over medium heat, cook bacon, onions and garlic until bacon is crisp, stirring occasionally. Stir in carrots and cabbage. Tie cloves and bay leaf in piece of cheese cloth or, if desired, place in tea ball. Add to cabbage mixture. Add bratwurst, partially covering with cabbage mixture. Pour beef broth and wine over cabbage mixture.

Bring to a boil. Reduce heat; cover and simmer 30 to 45 minutes or until vegetables are tender. Remove spices. Season to taste with salt and pepper. Serve with German-style or Dijon mustard and dark bread, if desired. 8 servings.

NUTRITION INFORMATION PER SERVING

SERVING SIZE: 1/8 OF RECIPE		PERCENT U.S. RDA PER SERVING	
CALORIES	340	PROTEIN	25%
PROTEIN	16 g	VITAMIN A	170%
CARBOHYDRATE	14 g	VITAMIN C	70%
FAT	24 g	THIAMINE	35%
CHOLESTEROL	54 mg	RIBOFLAVIN	10%
SODIUM	780 mg	NIACIN	20%
POTASSIUM	670 mg	CALCIUM	10%
		IRON	10%

Pictured on previous page: Quick Sausage Stew

You'll be surprised how quickly you can prepare this five-ingredient soup.

CHEESY VEGETABLE CHOWDER

3¼ cups milk
1 (10½-oz.) can condensed
   cream of potato soup
1 (10½-oz.) can condensed
   cream of celery soup
1 pkg. Green Giant® Creamy
   Cheddar Pasta Accents®
   Frozen Vegetables with
   Pasta
1 tablespoon grated Parmesan
   cheese

In large saucepan, combine milk and soups; mix well. Cook over medium heat until thoroughly heated. Meanwhile, prepare frozen vegetables with pasta as directed on package until vegetables are crisp-tender. Stir into soup mixture. Heat just to boiling, stirring occasionally. Sprinkle each serving with Parmesan cheese. 5 (1½-cup) servings.

MICROWAVE DIRECTIONS: Cook frozen vegetables with pasta in microwave according to package directions. Set aside. In 8-cup microwave-safe measuring cup, combine milk and soups; mix well. Microwave on HIGH for 7 to 9 minutes or until mixture is hot, stirring once halfway through cooking. Stir in cooked vegetables with pasta. Microwave on HIGH for 1 to 2 minutes or until thoroughly heated. Sprinkle each serving with Parmesan cheese.

TIP: For **tandem cooking,** prepare frozen vegetables with pasta according to microwave directions. Meanwhile, prepare soups according to conventional directions. Stir cooked vegetables with pasta into soup.

NUTRITION INFORMATION PER SERVING

SERVING SIZE: 1-1/2 CUPS		PERCENT U.S. RDA PER SERVING	
CALORIES	280	PROTEIN	20%
PROTEIN	12g	VITAMIN A	45%
CARBOHYDRATE	31g	VITAMIN C	20%
FAT	13g	THIAMINE	10%
CHOLESTEROL	33mg	RIBOFLAVIN	25%
SODIUM	1320mg	NIACIN	8%
POTASSIUM	520mg	CALCIUM	35%
		IRON	8%

Here's a perfect meal for a cool winter evening.

CHILI BEEF SKILLET

1 lb. ground beef
1 (16-oz.) can tomatoes,
   undrained, cut up
1 tablespoon flour
½ teaspoon chili powder
¼ teaspoon salt
1 (16-oz.) pkg. Green Giant®
   Garlic Seasoning Pasta
   Accents® Frozen Vegetables
   with Pasta
4 oz. (1 cup) shredded Cheddar
   cheese

Brown ground beef in large skillet; drain. In medium bowl, combine tomatoes, flour, chili powder and salt; blend well. Add tomato mixture and frozen vegetables with pasta to cooked ground beef in skillet; mix well. Bring to a boil. Stir; reduce heat and cover. Simmer 5 to 8 minutes or until vegetables are crisp-tender, stirring occasionally. Sprinkle with cheese. Cover; let stand 3 minutes or until cheese is melted. 5 servings.

NUTRITION INFORMATION PER SERVING

SERVING SIZE: 1/5 OF RECIPE		PERCENT U.S. RDA PER SERVING	
CALORIES	420	PROTEIN	40%
PROTEIN	25g	VITAMIN A	70%
CARBOHYDRATE	21g	VITAMIN C	35%
FAT	26g	THIAMINE	15%
CHOLESTEROL	91mg	RIBOFLAVIN	20%
SODIUM	780mg	NIACIN	30%
POTASSIUM	570mg	CALCIUM	25%
		IRON	15%

This native Hungarian dish is typically seasoned with paprika.

HUNGARIAN GOULASH

3 lb. boneless beef chuck, cut
    into 1-inch cubes
¼ cup flour
¼ cup oil
3 cups sliced onions
1 tablespoon paprika
1 teaspoon salt
⅛ teaspoon pepper
1 (10½-oz.) can condensed beef
    broth
1 (16-oz. pkg.) uncooked extra
    wide egg noodles
2 tablespoons margarine or
    butter
1 tablespoon poppy seed
1 cup dairy sour cream

In medium bowl, toss meat cubes
with flour to coat. In Dutch oven or
5-quart saucepan, brown meat in hot
oil. Add onions, paprika, salt, pepper
and beef broth; mix well. Cover;
simmer 1½ hours or until meat is
tender. Shortly before serving, cook
noodles to desired doneness as
directed on package. Drain; toss with
margarine and poppy seed.

Add sour cream to meat mixture.
Cook over low heat until thoroughly
heated, stirring constantly. Serve
goulash over hot cooked noodles.
8 to 10 servings.

NUTRITION INFORMATION PER SERVING

SERVING SIZE: 1/10 OF RECIPE		PERCENT U.S. RDA PER SERVING	
CALORIES	540	PROTEIN	60%
PROTEIN	40g	VITAMIN A	15%
CARBOHYDRATE	40g	VITAMIN C	2%
FAT	24g	THIAMINE	40%
CHOLESTEROL	146mg	RIBOFLAVIN	35%
SODIUM	480mg	NIACIN	40%
POTASSIUM	520mg	CALCIUM	6%
		IRON	35%

HAMBURGER FLORENTINE SOUP

(pictured on right)

1 lb. ground beef
5 cups water
2 cups cubed potatoes
1 cup shredded cabbage
1 cup chopped onions
1 cup sliced celery
⅓ cup uncooked barley
1½ teaspoons salt
½ teaspoon dried basil leaves
½ teaspoon dried thyme leaves
¼ teaspoon pepper
1 bay leaf
1 (28-oz.) can tomatoes,
    undrained, cut up
1 (14.5-oz.) can Green Giant®
    Kitchen Sliced® Green
    Beans, undrained
1 (9-oz.) pkg. Green Giant®
    Harvest Fresh® Frozen
    Chopped Spinach

Brown ground beef in 5-quart
saucepan or Dutch oven; drain. Stir in
all remaining ingredients except
spinach. Bring to a boil. Reduce heat;
cover and simmer 30 minutes. Add
frozen spinach; cover and simmer an
additional 25 minutes. Stir to blend
spinach into soup. Remove bay leaf.
11 (1⅓-cup) servings.

NUTRITION INFORMATION PER SERVING

SERVING SIZE: 1-1/3 CUPS		PERCENT U.S. RDA PER SERVING	
CALORIES	160	PROTEIN	15%
PROTEIN	10g	VITAMIN A	20%
CARBOHYDRATE	16g	VITAMIN C	35%
FAT	6g	THIAMINE	8%
CHOLESTEROL	25mg	RIBOFLAVIN	8%
SODIUM	570mg	NIACIN	15%
POTASSIUM	630mg	CALCIUM	6%
		IRON	15%

COOK'S NOTE
BARLEY
Barley is a hearty grain and one of
the first grains used as food, even
predating wheat. Pearl barley has
the outer bran removed and is
polished. It is the form most
prevalent today and is used as a
healthful ingredient in soups,
breads, salads and main dishes.

HERBED BUTTERMILK STROGANOFF

¾ lb. boneless beef round steak, cut into 3x¼-inch strips
1 cup sliced fresh mushrooms
1 cup sliced onions
½ cup water
⅓ cup dry white wine or beef broth
3 tablespoons tomato juice
1 teaspoon beef-flavor instant bouillon
½ teaspoon salt
¼ teaspoon dried thyme leaves
¼ teaspoon dried rosemary leaves
⅛ teaspoon pepper
2 tablespoons flour
¾ cup lowfat buttermilk
Hot cooked noodles
2 tablespoons chopped fresh parsley

Spray large non-stick skillet with cooking spray; heat over medium-high heat until hot. Add beef, mushrooms and onions. Cook until beef is lightly browned; drain, if necessary. Stir in water, wine, tomato juice, bouillon, salt, thyme, rosemary and pepper. Reduce heat; cover and simmer 45 minutes or until meat is tender, stirring occasionally.

In small bowl, whisk flour with ¼ cup of the buttermilk until smooth; whisk in remaining ½ cup buttermilk. Stir into beef mixture. Cook over medium heat until thickened, stirring constantly. Serve over hot cooked noodles; sprinkle with parsley. 5 servings.

NUTRITION INFORMATION PER SERVING

SERVING SIZE: 1/5 OF RECIPE		PERCENT U.S. RDA PER SERVING	
CALORIES	350	PROTEIN	35%
PROTEIN	22g	VITAMIN A	2%
CARBOHYDRATE	47g	VITAMIN C	8%
FAT	7g	THIAMINE	25%
CHOLESTEROL	90mg	RIBOFLAVIN	20%
SODIUM	390mg	NIACIN	25%
POTASSIUM	420mg	CALCIUM	8%
		IRON	25%

SWEDISH MEATBALLS

½ lb. ground beef
½ lb. ground pork
½ lb. ground veal
¾ cup chopped onions
1 tablespoon margarine or butter
¾ cup soft bread crumbs
½ cup milk
1 teaspoon salt
¼ teaspoon pepper
¼ teaspoon allspice
1 egg
¼ cup flour
1½ cups chicken broth
1½ cups half-and-half
6 cups uncooked extra wide egg noodles

In large bowl, combine ground beef, pork and veal. In large skillet, cook and stir onions in margarine until tender. Add onions, bread crumbs, milk, salt, pepper, allspice and egg to the meat; mix well. If desired, refrigerate for easier handling. Shape into 1½-inch balls.

In same skillet over medium heat, cook meatballs, turning carefully to brown evenly. Remove meatballs from skillet, reserving 2 tablespoons meat drippings in skillet. Stir in flour; cook until mixture is smooth and bubbly, stirring constantly. Gradually add chicken broth. Cook until mixture boils and thickens, stirring constantly. Stir in half-and-half; cook an additional 2 minutes. Add meatballs to sauce; simmer 10 minutes, stirring occasionally. Meanwhile, cook noodles as directed on package; drain. Serve meatballs and sauce over hot cooked noodles. 6 servings.

TIP: Three-fourths lb. ground beef and ¾ lb. ground pork can be used; omit veal.

NUTRITION INFORMATION PER SERVING

SERVING SIZE: 1/6 OF RECIPE		PERCENT U.S. RDA PER SERVING	
CALORIES	510	PROTEIN	50%
PROTEIN	31g	VITAMIN A	8%
CARBOHYDRATE	40g	VITAMIN C	2%
FAT	25g	THIAMINE	45%
CHOLESTEROL	171mg	RIBOFLAVIN	35%
SODIUM	720mg	NIACIN	45%
POTASSIUM	570mg	CALCIUM	10%
		IRON	20%

This family favorite is ready in under 30 minutes.

CHOW MEIN

1 lb. chow mein meat or ground
beef
1½ cups water
2 tablespoons soy sauce
½ teaspoon ginger
1 beef-flavor bouillon cube or
1 teaspoon beef-flavor
instant bouillon
1½ cups sliced celery
1 (16-oz.) can bean sprouts,
drained
1 (8-oz.) can sliced water
chestnuts, drained
1 (4-oz.) can Green Giant®
Mushrooms Pieces and
Stems, drained
2 tablespoons cornstarch
2 tablespoons water
4 cups chow mein noodles or
hot cooked rice

Brown meat in large skillet; drain.
Add 1½ cups water, soy sauce, ginger,
bouillon cube, celery, bean sprouts,
water chestnuts and mushrooms; mix
well. Cover and simmer 15 minutes,
stirring occasionally.

In small bowl, blend cornstarch and
2 tablespoons water until smooth. Stir
into meat mixture; cook until
mixture thickens and boils. Serve
over chow mein noodles or hot rice.
3 to 4 servings.

▤ MICROWAVE DIRECTIONS:
Place meat in 2-quart microwave-safe
casserole. Microwave on HIGH for
4 to 5½ minutes or until meat is no
longer pink, stirring once halfway
through cooking; drain.

Add bouillon cube, celery, bean
sprouts, water chestnuts and
mushrooms. In small bowl, combine
1 cup water, soy sauce and ginger;
stir into meat mixture. Cover;
microwave on HIGH for 8 minutes,
stirring once halfway through
cooking.

In small bowl, blend cornstarch and
2 tablespoons water until smooth. Stir
into meat mixture. Microwave on
HIGH for 4 to 5½ minutes or until
mixture thickens and boils, stirring
twice during cooking. Serve over
chow mein noodles or hot rice.

NUTRITION INFORMATION PER SERVING

SERVING SIZE: 1/4 OF RECIPE		PERCENT U.S. RDA PER SERVING	
CALORIES	550	PROTEIN	40%
PROTEIN	27 g	VITAMIN A	2%
CARBOHYDRATE	43 g	VITAMIN C	6%
FAT	31 g	THIAMINE	40%
CHOLESTEROL	74 mg	RIBOFLAVIN	30%
SODIUM	1180 mg	NIACIN	40%
POTASSIUM	710 mg	CALCIUM	4%
		IRON	25%

Zesty salsa, a combination of tomatoes, roasted green chiles and onions, is just one of many culinary delights that come to us from Mexico. For a change of pace, top meat loaf slices with salsa, shredded lettuce and sour cream.

SALSA MEAT LOAF

1 lb. lean ground beef or ground
turkey
½ cup quick-cooking rolled oats
1 teaspoon dried basil leaves
½ teaspoon dried oregano leaves
¼ teaspoon salt, if desired
⅛ teaspoon pepper
½ cup thick and chunky salsa
1 egg, slightly beaten

Heat oven to 350°F. In large bowl,
combine all ingredients; mix well. In
ungreased 9-inch square pan, shape
meat mixture into 7x3½-inch loaf.
Bake at 350°F for 50 to 60 minutes or
until meat is well browned and firm.
Let stand 5 minutes before slicing. If
desired, serve with any remaining
salsa. 4 servings.

TIP: Meat loaf can be baked in ungreased
8x4-inch loaf pan.

NUTRITION INFORMATION PER SERVING

SERVING SIZE: 1/4 OF RECIPE		PERCENT U.S. RDA PER SERVING	
CALORIES	290	PROTEIN	35%
PROTEIN	23 g	VITAMIN A	4%
CARBOHYDRATE	10 g	VITAMIN C	*
FAT	17 g	THIAMINE	8%
CHOLESTEROL	123 mg	RIBOFLAVIN	15%
SODIUM	430 mg	NIACIN	20%
POTASSIUM	380 mg	CALCIUM	4%
		IRON	15%

*Contains less than 2% of the U.S. RDA of this nutrient.

Colby/Monterey jack cheese is a marbled blend of two cheeses and can be found in both bulk and shredded form.

CHEESY NOODLE CASSEROLE

(pictured on left)

8 oz. (5 cups) uncooked
   dumpling noodles
1½ lb. ground turkey
1 medium onion, chopped
1 (15-oz.) jar prepared spaghetti
   sauce
1 (10¾-oz.) can condensed
   Cheddar cheese soup
1 (8-oz.) can tomato sauce
1 (4-oz.) can Green Giant®
   Mushrooms Pieces and
   Stems, drained
¼ teaspoon garlic powder
¼ teaspoon dried thyme leaves
¼ teaspoon pepper
8 oz. (2 cups) shredded colby/
   Monterey jack cheese or
   Cheddar cheese

Cook noodles to desired doneness as directed on package. Drain; rinse with hot water. Place in large bowl.

Heat oven to 350°F. In large skillet over medium-high heat, brown ground turkey and onion; drain, if necessary. Stir in remaining ingredients except cheese and noodles; simmer 3 to 4 minutes. Pour turkey mixture over noodles; mix well. Pour into ungreased 13x9-inch (3-quart) baking dish. Cover; bake at 350°F. for 35 to 40 minutes or until hot and bubbly. Uncover; sprinkle with cheese. Bake uncovered an additional 5 minutes or until cheese is melted. 8 to 10 servings.

NUTRITION INFORMATION PER SERVING

SERVING SIZE: 1/10 OF RECIPE		PERCENT U.S. RDA PER SERVING	
CALORIES	380	PROTEIN	35%
PROTEIN	23g	VITAMIN A	25%
CARBOHYDRATE	29g	VITAMIN C	10%
FAT	19g	THIAMINE	20%
CHOLESTEROL	83mg	RIBOFLAVIN	20%
SODIUM	790mg	NIACIN	25%
POTASSIUM	550mg	CALCIUM	25%
		IRON	15%

Easy as one, two, three! Three ingredients are used for this creamy pasta dish, which continues to rate high in popularity with children.

STOVETOP MACARONI AND CHEESE

1 cup uncooked elbow macaroni
¾ cup milk
8 oz. pasteurized processed
   cheese spread, cubed

Cook macaroni to desired doneness as directed on package. Drain; rinse with hot water.

In same saucepan, combine cooked macaroni, milk and cheese. Cook over medium heat until cheese melts and sauce is smooth, stirring occasionally. Let stand 3 to 5 minutes before serving. 2 to 3 servings.

🖳 MICROWAVE DIRECTIONS: Prepare macaroni as directed above. In 8-cup microwave-safe measuring cup, combine cooked macaroni, milk and cheese. Microwave on HIGH for 4 to 5 minutes or until cheese melts and sauce is smooth, stirring once halfway through cooking. Let stand 5 minutes before serving.

NUTRITION INFORMATION PER SERVING

SERVING SIZE: 1/3 OF RECIPE		PERCENT U.S. RDA PER SERVING	
CALORIES	350	PROTEIN	30%
PROTEIN	18g	VITAMIN A	15%
CARBOHYDRATE	30g	VITAMIN C	*
FAT	18g	THIAMINE	25%
CHOLESTEROL	46mg	RIBOFLAVIN	30%
SODIUM	1050mg	NIACIN	10%
POTASSIUM	320mg	CALCIUM	50%
		IRON	8%

*Contains less than 2% of the U.S. RDA of this nutrient.

Cheesy Noodle Casserole

This flavorful stovetop version of "baked" beans has no molasses or ketchup.

BEAN AND BACON COMBO

(pictured above)

½ lb. (1¼ cups) dried baby lima
    beans*
½ lb. (1 cup) dried navy beans*
 8 cups water
½ lb. bacon, cut into 1-inch
    pieces
 1 cup chopped onions
½ cup sliced celery including
    leaves
 1 garlic clove, minced
 1 (16-oz.) can tomatoes,
    undrained, cut up
 2 tablespoons brown sugar
½ teaspoon ginger
½ teaspoon salt
 1 tablespoon prepared mustard
 1 tablespoon Worcestershire
    sauce

Sort and wash beans. Place in 5-quart saucepan or Dutch oven. Cover with water. Bring to a boil; boil gently for 2 minutes. Remove from heat; cover and let stand 1 hour. Bring to a second boil. Reduce heat and simmer about 30 minutes or until beans are tender. Drain liquid, reserving ½ cup.**

Cook bacon in large skillet or 5-quart saucepan until crisp. Remove from skillet; drain on paper towels. Reserve 2 tablespoons cooked bacon.

Drain bacon drippings, reserving 2 tablespoons in skillet. Cook onions, celery and garlic in drippings until tender. Stir in tomatoes, brown sugar, ginger, salt, mustard, Worcestershire sauce and remaining cooked bacon. Simmer for 15 minutes, stirring occasionally. Stir in beans. If bean mixture is too dry, gradually add ½ cup reserved liquid until of desired consistency. Cook over medium heat until thoroughly heated. Just before

serving, sprinkle with reserved
2 tablespoons cooked bacon.
8 (1-cup) servings.

TIPS: *Two 15.5-oz. cans lima beans,
         drained, reserving ½ cup liquid,
         and two 16-oz. cans navy or Great
         Northern beans, drained, can be
         substituted for the dried beans.
         Omit first paragraph of recipe.

         **An alternative method for
         hydrating beans is covering them
         with water and soaking them
         overnight. To cook, bring to a
         boil. Reduce heat and simmer
         about 30 minutes or until beans
         are tender. Drain liquid, reserving
         ½ cup. Continue as directed in
         second paragraph of recipe.

Pictured left to right: Bean and Bacon Combo,
Hearty Grain Quick Loaf p. 42

COOK'S NOTE
DRIED BEANS
Dried beans are one of the oldest
known foods, dating back 4000
years. They are generally soaked
in water to rehydrate before being
cooked. Nutritionally, they are
rich in protein, calcium,
phosphorus, potassium and iron.
Store dried beans in an airtight
container in a dry place.

NUTRITION INFORMATION PER SERVING

SERVING SIZE: 1 CUP		PERCENT U.S. RDA PER SERVING	
CALORIES	300	PROTEIN	25%
PROTEIN	16g	VITAMIN A	6%
CARBOHYDRATE	44g	VITAMIN C	15%
FAT	8g	THIAMINE	30%
CHOLESTEROL	10mg	RIBOFLAVIN	10%
SODIUM	410mg	NIACIN	10%
POTASSIUM	1050mg	CALCIUM	10%
		IRON	25%

Lean pork and colorful crisp peppers combine in this attractive and flavorful entree. Serve it with rice or Oriental noodles if desired.

PORK AND PEPPERS STIR-FRY

(pictured on right)

1 lb. pork tenderloin, cut into
    thin strips
1 tablespoon sugar
2 tablespoons soy sauce
1 tablespoon fresh gingerroot,
    minced, or 1½ teaspoons
    ground ginger
1 to 2 garlic cloves, minced
2 tablespoons oil
1 medium green bell pepper, cut
    into ¼-inch strips
1 medium red bell pepper, cut
    into ¼-inch strips
1 medium yellow bell pepper,
    cut into ¼-inch strips
1 green onion, sliced
1 (8-oz.) can pineapple chunks
    in its own juice, reserving
    liquid
1 tablespoon cornstarch
½ teaspoon brown sugar
1 teaspoon soy sauce

In medium bowl, combine pork, sugar, 2 tablespoons soy sauce, gingerroot and garlic; mix well. Let stand 15 minutes to blend flavors. Heat 12-inch skillet over medium-high heat until hot. Add 1 tablespoon of the oil; heat oil until it ripples. Add pork mixture; stir-fry for 3 minutes or until pork is no longer pink. Remove from skillet. Add remaining 1 table-spoon oil. Stir-fry peppers and onion in hot oil 3 minutes or until crisp-tender.

In small bowl, combine reserved pineapple liquid, cornstarch, brown sugar and 1 teaspoon soy sauce; blend well. Add cooked pork and pineapple to skillet. Stir in cornstarch mixture. Cook until sauce is thickened and pineapple is thoroughly heated, stirring constantly. 4 to 6 servings.

NUTRITION INFORMATION PER SERVING

SERVING SIZE: 1/6 OF RECIPE		PERCENT U.S. RDA PER SERVING	
CALORIES	190	PROTEIN	30%
PROTEIN	18g	VITAMIN A	20%
CARBOHYDRATE	13g	VITAMIN C	60%
FAT	8g	THIAMINE	40%
CHOLESTEROL	55mg	RIBOFLAVIN	15%
SODIUM	440mg	NIACIN	15%
POTASSIUM	460mg	CALCIUM	*
		IRON	8%

*Contains less than 2% of the U.S. RDA of this nutrient.

We think you will agree that these ribs are "finger-lickin'" good.

BAKED RIBS AND SAUERKRAUT

3 lb. spareribs or country-style
    ribs
1½ teaspoons salt
¼ teaspoon pepper
1 (32-oz.) jar sauerkraut,
    undrained
¼ cup water
2 tablespoons brown sugar
2 tart apples, peeled, chopped
1 small onion, chopped

Heat oven to 450°F. Cut ribs into serving-sized pieces. Place in ungreased 13x9-inch pan; sprinkle with salt and pepper. Bake at 450°F. for 20 minutes.

Reduce oven temperature to 350°F. Remove ribs from pan; drain drippings from pan. In same pan, combine sauerkraut and remaining ingredients; spread evenly over bottom. Arrange ribs on top of sauerkraut mixture. Bake at 350°F. for 1½ to 2 hours or until ribs are tender, stirring occasionally. 5 to 6 servings.

NUTRITION INFORMATION PER SERVING

SERVING SIZE: 1/6 OF RECIPE		PERCENT U.S. RDA PER SERVING	
CALORIES	410	PROTEIN	40%
PROTEIN	27g	VITAMIN A	*
CARBOHYDRATE	15g	VITAMIN C	20%
FAT	27g	THIAMINE	25%
CHOLESTEROL	107mg	RIBOFLAVIN	20%
SODIUM	1220mg	NIACIN	25%
POTASSIUM	520mg	CALCIUM	8%
		IRON	20%

*Contains less than 2% of the U.S. RDA of this nutrient.

Pork and Peppers Stir-Fry

LASAGNA ROLL-UPS

We cut the calories, fat and sodium...
but saved the great taste!

For vigilant waist-watchers, lasagna—layered with plenty of cheese—may be just too much of a good thing. *Lasagna Roll-Ups,* our 1990s make-over of *Classic Italian Lasagna,* makes this favorite recipe with fewer calories and less fat and sodium while keeping good old-fashioned taste.

Made with ground turkey, lowfat ricotta or cottage cheese and spinach, each roll-up weighs in at a slim 350 calories, compared to 550 calories per serving in the classic version. And, by cutting the fat content nearly in half, we've reduced the calories derived from fat from 43 to 36 percent. Sodium level is reduced from 1,400 to 840mg per serving of *Lasagna Roll-Ups.* Make-over or original, the choice is yours!

Lasagna Roll-Ups

You may not think of lasagna as a low-calorie entree, but here it is! Our version is done in a pretty rolled-up shape and is a good source of calcium and vitamins A and C.

LASAGNA ROLL-UPS

(pictured on left)

SAUCE
½ lb. ground turkey
2 garlic cloves, minced
1 (32-oz.) jar prepared spaghetti
    sauce
2 teaspoons dried Italian
    seasoning
½ teaspoon fennel seed, if
    desired

FILLING
8 uncooked lasagna noodles
1 cup lowfat part-skim ricotta or
    cottage cheese
½ cup shredded carrot
1 (9-oz.) pkg. Green Giant®
    Harvest Fresh® Frozen
    Chopped Spinach, thawed,
    squeezed dry
2 egg whites or 1 egg
¼ teaspoon salt

TOPPING
4 oz. (1 cup) shredded lowfat
    part-skim mozzarella cheese

Heat oven to 350°F. In large skillet, brown turkey and garlic; drain, if necessary. Stir in remaining sauce ingredients; simmer about 15 minutes, stirring occasionally. Meanwhile, cook lasagna noodles to desired doneness as directed on package. Drain; rinse with hot water.

In small bowl, combine ricotta cheese, carrot, spinach, egg whites and salt; mix well. Spread each cooked lasagna noodle with generous ¼ cup spinach filling to within 1 inch of 1 short end. Roll up firmly toward unfilled end.

Reserve 1½ cups of sauce. Pour remaining sauce in ungreased 12x8-inch (2-quart) baking dish. Arrange roll-ups, seam side down, in sauce. Pour reserved sauce over roll-ups. Cover; bake at 350°F. for 30 to 40 minutes or until hot and bubbly. Sprinkle with mozzarella cheese. Bake uncovered an additional 3 to 5 minutes or until cheese is melted. Let stand 5 minutes before serving. 8 servings.

NUTRITION INFORMATION PER SERVING

SERVING SIZE: 1/8 OF RECIPE		PERCENT U.S. RDA PER SERVING	
CALORIES	350	PROTEIN	30%
PROTEIN	19g	VITAMIN A	80%
CARBOHYDRATE	38g	VITAMIN C	25%
FAT	14g	THIAMINE	20%
CHOLESTEROL	31mg	RIBOFLAVIN	25%
SODIUM	840mg	NIACIN	25%
POTASSIUM	780mg	CALCIUM	25%
		IRON	15%

Serve this hearty Italian dish with garlic breadsticks, Winter Green Salad (see Index) and raspberry sherbet.

CLASSIC ITALIAN LASAGNA

6 uncooked lasagna noodles

MEAT SAUCE
½ lb. bulk Italian sausage
½ cup chopped onion
1 (4-oz.) can Green Giant®
    Mushrooms Pieces and
    Stems, drained
1½ cups finely chopped cooked
    chicken
1 (16-oz.) jar prepared spaghetti
    sauce

CHEESE FILLING
1 (15-oz.) container ricotta
    cheese
1 (9-oz.) pkg. Green Giant®
    Harvest Fresh® Frozen
    Chopped Spinach, thawed,
    squeezed to drain
½ cup grated Parmesan cheese
2 eggs, beaten

8 oz. sliced or 2 cups shredded
    mozzarella cheese

continued on p. 20

continued from p. 19

Cook lasagna noodles to desired doneness as directed on package. Drain; rinse with hot water.

Heat oven to 350°F. Lightly grease 12x8-inch (2-quart) baking dish. In medium skillet, brown sausage and onion, breaking sausage into small pieces. Remove from skillet; drain on paper towel. In large bowl, combine sausage mixture, mushrooms, chicken and spaghetti sauce; mix well. In small bowl, combine all cheese filling ingredients; mix well.

In greased dish, layer ½ of cooked noodles, ½ of meat sauce, ½ of cheese filling and ½ of mozzarella cheese; repeat layers, ending with mozzarella cheese on top.

Bake at 350°F. for 30 to 35 minutes or until hot and bubbly. Let stand 10 to 15 minutes before serving. 6 servings.

NUTRITION INFORMATION PER SERVING

SERVING SIZE: 1/6 OF RECIPE		PERCENT U.S. RDA PER SERVING	
CALORIES	550	PROTEIN	70%
PROTEIN	43g	VITAMIN A	30%
CARBOHYDRATE	35g	VITAMIN C	4%
FAT	26g	THIAMINE	25%
CHOLESTEROL	180mg	RIBOFLAVIN	35%
SODIUM	1400mg	NIACIN	25%
POTASSIUM	550mg	CALCIUM	70%
		IRON	20%

COOK'S NOTE
BEEF-PORK ROLLED ROAST

A beef-pork combination roast is created from two cuts of meat, beef sirloin tip and pork loin, which are rolled and tied together into a roast. If one is not readily available at your meat counter, ask the butcher to prepare it for you. A new taste is created for a delicious change of pace by combining the flavors of beef and pork in one roast.

An herbed marinade imparts a sensational flavor to this rolled roast and is a great low calorie alternative to rich gravies. Try this new cut of meat for a delicious way to enjoy two meats rolled into one! For your next down-home family meal, serve this roast with Winter Vegetables with Rosemary (see Index).

HERB-MARINATED ROAST

(pictured on p. 48)

MARINADE
½ cup burgundy or dry red wine
¼ cup lemon juice
1 (8-oz.) can tomato sauce
1 tablespoon prepared mustard
1 teaspoon dried thyme leaves
¼ teaspoon dried oregano leaves
¼ teaspoon pepper

ROAST
1 (3-lb.) boneless rolled beef-pork combination roast or sirloin tip roast

In small bowl, combine all marinade ingredients. Place roast in large non-metal bowl or plastic bag; pour marinade over roast. Cover bowl or seal bag; marinate in refrigerator 8 hours or overnight, turning roast occasionally.

Heat oven to 325°F. Place roast and marinade in ungreased roasting pan. Insert meat thermometer. Cover; bake at 325°F. for 1½ to 2 hours or until meat thermometer registers 165°F., basting occasionally with marinade.* Uncover; let stand 15 minutes before slicing. Skim fat from marinade; serve marinade with roast. 8 to 10 servings.

TIP: *Bake sirloin tip roast as directed above until meat thermometer registers 150°F.

NUTRITION INFORMATION PER SERVING

SERVING SIZE: 1/10 OF RECIPE		PERCENT U.S. RDA PER SERVING	
CALORIES	260	PROTEIN	45%
PROTEIN	31g	VITAMIN A	4%
CARBOHYDRATE	2g	VITAMIN C	4%
FAT	12g	THIAMINE	35%
CHOLESTEROL	95mg	RIBOFLAVIN	20%
SODIUM	230mg	NIACIN	30%
POTASSIUM	520mg	CALCIUM	2%
		IRON	15%

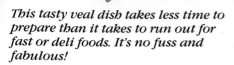

This tasty veal dish takes less time to prepare than it takes to run out for fast or deli foods. It's no fuss and fabulous!

VEAL WITH MUSHROOM PECAN SAUCE

½ cup grated Parmesan cheese
3 tablespoons crushed
    cornflakes cereal
4 boneless veal cutlets (1 to
    1½ lb.)
1 egg, beaten
2 tablespoons margarine or
    butter
¾ cup sliced fresh mushrooms
1 tablespoon sliced green onions
1 tablespoon flour
¼ teaspoon salt
¼ teaspoon dried thyme leaves
¼ teaspoon dry mustard
1 cup half-and-half
¼ cup coarsely chopped pecans,
    toasted*
1 (10-oz.) pkg. Green Giant® Rice
    Originals® Frozen Long
    Grain White and Wild Rice
2 tablespoons oil

In shallow dish, combine Parmesan cheese and crushed cereal. Dip veal in egg; coat with cereal mixture. Set aside.

To prepare sauce, melt margarine in small saucepan over medium heat. Add mushrooms and onions; cook and stir until vegetables are tender. Stir in flour, salt, thyme and mustard. Cook until mixture is smooth and bubbly, stirring constantly. Gradually add half-and-half. Cook until mixture boils and thickens, stirring constantly. Boil 1 minute, stirring constantly. Stir in pecans. Cover; keep warm.

Prepare rice as directed on package. Meanwhile, in large skillet over medium heat, cook veal in hot oil about 5 minutes on each side or until browned. To serve, place each veal cutlet on plate; spoon about ⅓ cup cooked rice over veal. Serve with Mushroom Pecan Sauce. 4 servings.

    📠 MICROWAVE DIRECTIONS: To prepare sauce, place margarine in 4-cup microwave-safe measuring cup. Microwave on HIGH for 20 to 30 seconds or until melted. Add mushrooms and onions. Microwave on HIGH for 45 to 60 seconds or until vegetables are tender. Stir in flour, salt, thyme, mustard and half-and-half; blend well. Microwave on HIGH for 3 to 3½ minutes or until mixture boils and thickens, stirring once during cooking. Stir in pecans.

TIP: *To toast pecans, spread pecans on
      cookie sheet; bake at 350°F. for 5 to
      7 minutes or until golden brown,
      stirring occasionally.

NUTRITION INFORMATION PER SERVING

SERVING SIZE: 1/4 OF RECIPE		PERCENT U.S. RDA PER SERVING	
CALORIES	600	PROTEIN	60%
PROTEIN	40g	VITAMIN A	15%
CARBOHYDRATE	26g	VITAMIN C	4%
FAT	38g	THIAMINE	20%
CHOLESTEROL	203mg	RIBOFLAVIN	40%
SODIUM	860mg	NIACIN	70%
POTASSIUM	620mg	CALCIUM	25%
		IRON	15%

COOK'S NOTE
FENNEL

Fennel is an aromatic vegetable with a broad bulbous base, celery-like stems and green feathery foliage. Fennel is similar in flavor to anise although sweeter and more delicate.

To prepare fennel, cut off most of the green foliage and run water between the stems. Both the base and stems can be eaten raw in salads or cooked in a variety of methods such as braising, sauteing or steaming. Fragrant and graceful, the greens can be used as a garnish.

A whiff of the aroma this roast produces as it bakes may take you back to grandma's kitchen.

ROAST PORK LOIN WITH SAVORY STUFFING

SAVORY STUFFING
1 cup dry herb-seasoned stuffing
3 tablespoons margarine or
    butter, melted
½ cup chopped onion
½ cup chopped celery including
    leaves
1 (4-oz.) can Green Giant®
    Mushrooms Pieces and
    Stems, drained
¼ cup chopped walnuts
⅛ teaspoon dried thyme leaves
⅛ teaspoon fennel seed

ROAST
1 (3 to 3½-lb.) tied boneless pork
    loin roast
    Salt and pepper

Heat oven to 325°F. Grease shallow roasting pan. In medium bowl, combine herb stuffing and margarine; mix well. Stir in remaining stuffing ingredients. Untie roast; separate into halves. Spread stuffing mixture on bottom half; replace top half. Using wooden picks or metal skewers, secure stuffed roast well on all sides, or retie. Place in greased roasting pan; salt and pepper top of roast. Insert meat thermometer.

Roast at 325°F. for 1½ to 2 hours or until meat thermometer registers 160°F. Let stand 10 minutes before slicing. 8 to 10 servings.

NUTRITION INFORMATION PER SERVING

SERVING SIZE: 1/10 OF RECIPE		PERCENT U.S. RDA PER SERVING	
CALORIES	380	PROTEIN	50%
PROTEIN	35g	VITAMIN A	2%
CARBOHYDRATE	7g	VITAMIN C	*
FAT	23g	THIAMINE	70%
CHOLESTEROL	113mg	RIBOFLAVIN	30%
SODIUM	300mg	NIACIN	40%
POTASSIUM	530mg	CALCIUM	2%
		IRON	10%

*Contains less than 2% of the U.S. RDA of this nutrient.

The fruit in this stuffing assures a delightful burst of flavor with each bite. Whether for company or family, this entree will be a hit.

APPLE APRICOT STUFFED PORK CHOPS

(pictured on right)

6 loin pork chops, 1 inch thick
½ cup chopped onion
½ cup chopped celery
1 tablespoon margarine or
    butter
½ cup soft bread crumbs
½ cup chopped apple
⅓ cup golden or dark raisins
1 tablespoon brown sugar
½ teaspoon ginger
¼ cup apricot preserves

Heat oven to 325°F. Cut deep horizontal pocket in each chop. In medium skillet, cook onion and celery in margarine until crisp-tender. Add bread crumbs, apple, raisins, brown sugar, ginger and 2 tablespoons of the preserves; mix well. Stuff each chop with about ¼ cup stuffing mixture. Place in ungreased 13x9-inch (3-quart) baking dish; cover.

Bake at 325°F. for 45 minutes. Uncover; spread top of chops with remaining 2 tablespoons preserves. Bake uncovered an additional 15 to 20 minutes or until pork chops are tender. 6 servings.

NUTRITION INFORMATION PER SERVING

SERVING SIZE: 1/6 OF RECIPE		PERCENT U.S. RDA PER SERVING	
CALORIES	270	PROTEIN	30%
PROTEIN	19g	VITAMIN A	2%
CARBOHYDRATE	22g	VITAMIN C	2%
FAT	12g	THIAMINE	40%
CHOLESTEROL	62mg	RIBOFLAVIN	15%
SODIUM	100mg	NIACIN	20%
POTASSIUM	400mg	CALCIUM	2%
		IRON	6%

Apple Apricot Stuffed Pork Chops

CLASSIC Pillsbury KNOW-HOW™
POT ROAST AND GRAVY
"Comfort food"—so easy to make

Pot roast and gravy ranks high among home cooked favorites. And it *is* something that you can make with our recipe and these easy step-by-step instructions.

Step 1. Browning helps develop the flavor and enhance the color of beef for pot roast. To brown meat, heat oil over medium-high heat in Dutch oven or roasting pan. Brown meat about 5 minutes on each side, turning roast with tongs or 2 large spoons to avoid piercing it. Drain excess fat, if desired. Add seasonings and cooking liquid. Bring to a boil. Cover; bake at 325°F. for 60 minutes.

Step 2. Add vegetables. If desired, insert meat thermometer into thickest part of meat. Cover again; bake 60 to 75 minutes or until meat and vegetables are fork tender. When meat and vegetables are tender, place them on a warm platter and cover to keep warm.

On a meat thermometer, pot roast is done at 208 to 212°F.

Use wire whisk for smoothest gravy

Step 3.
To make gravy, measure drippings and if desired, skim off fat. Add reserved broth to make 3 cups and return to Dutch oven. In a small jar with lid, shake flour and cold water until smooth. Gradually stir flour mixture into hot liquid. Cook and stir until gravy thickens and boils. Season to taste.

Step 4. (right) To serve *Pot Roast and Gravy,* **slice roast across the grain of the meat into thin slices.** Arrange vegetables around roast or place in a separate serving dish. Pour gravy into a serving bowl.Follow these simple directions for tender, juicy meat and succulent vegetables to cover with smooth, flavorful gravy. Comfort food at its best!

*This recipe reminds one of "home."
Serve it for a special family meal, or
use it as a reason to invite friends
for dinner.*

POT ROAST AND GRAVY

2 tablespoons oil
1 (3 to 4-lb.) beef chuck arm,
    blade or 7-bone pot roast
½ teaspoon pepper
4 medium onions, quartered
4 celery stalks, cut into pieces
1 bay leaf
2 beef-flavor bouillon cubes or
    2 teaspoons beef-flavor
    instant bouillon
1½ cups boiling water
6 medium potatoes, halved
6 medium carrots, cut into
    pieces
3 tablespoons flour
¼ cup cold water
    Salt to taste

Heat oven to 325°F. In 5-quart Dutch oven or roasting pan, heat oil over medium-high heat; brown meat about 5 minutes on each side. Drain excess fat, if desired. Sprinkle pepper on both sides of meat. Add 1 of the onions, 1 of the celery stalks and bay leaf to meat. Dissolve bouillon cubes in boiling water; reserve ¾ cup. Pour remaining ¾ cup of bouillon around meat. Bring to a boil; cover. Bake at 325°F. for 60 minutes. Add remaining vegetables; cover and bake an additional 60 to 75 minutes or until meat and vegetables are tender.

To prepare gravy, place meat and vegetables on warm platter; cover loosely to keep warm. Measure drippings from Dutch oven. Skim off fat, if desired. Add reserved ¾ cup bouillon to drippings to make 3 cups; return to Dutch oven. In small jar with tight-fitting lid, add flour to cold water; shake well. Gradually stir into drippings. Cook over medium heat until mixture boils and thickens, stirring constantly. Salt to taste. Serve with meat and vegetables. 6 servings.

NUTRITION INFORMATION PER SERVING

SERVING SIZE: 1/6 OF RECIPE		PERCENT U.S. RDA PER SERVING	
CALORIES	520	PROTEIN	80%
PROTEIN	49g	VITAMIN A	410%
CARBOHYDRATE	38g	VITAMIN C	40%
FAT	18g	THIAMINE	25%
CHOLESTEROL	136mg	RIBOFLAVIN	30%
SODIUM	520mg	NIACIN	40%
POTASSIUM	1430mg	CALCIUM	6%
		IRON	40%

Pot Roast and Gravy

Sometimes known as "smothered steak," this dish is always made with beef. Our version, with added vegetables, adds extra flavor and texture.

SWISS STEAK

1 (2 to 2½-lb.) beef round steak
   (½ to ¾ inch thick)
¼ cup flour
1 teaspoon salt
¼ teaspoon pepper
1 to 2 tablespoons oil
1 large onion, sliced
1 (8-oz.) can (1 cup) tomatoes,
   undrained, cut up*
1 (8-oz.) can tomato sauce*

Cut meat into serving-sized pieces. In small bowl, combine flour, salt and pepper. Toss meat with seasoned flour to coat, using all of the flour. In large skillet, brown meat in hot oil. Add remaining ingredients. Cover; simmer 1¼ to 1½ hours or until meat is tender. Serve with hot cooked potatoes or noodles, if desired. 6 servings.

TIPS: *One (10½-oz.) can condensed tomato soup and ½ cup water can be substituted for tomatoes and tomato sauce.

Peas, beans or mushrooms can be added to the Swiss Steak. Add peas and beans toward end of cooking; add mushrooms with onion.

NUTRITION INFORMATION PER SERVING

SERVING SIZE: 1/6 OF RECIPE		PERCENT U.S. RDA PER SERVING	
CALORIES	520	PROTEIN	45%
PROTEIN	29g	VITAMIN A	10%
CARBOHYDRATE	11g	VITAMIN C	15%
FAT	40g	THIAMINE	10%
CHOLESTEROL	103mg	RIBOFLAVIN	15%
SODIUM	730mg	NIACIN	25%
POTASSIUM	670mg	CALCIUM	4%
		IRON	20%

Serve this entree for a special occasion or for a fun family get-together. You'll appreciate the easy preparation.

CHICKEN CRANBERRY BAKE

(pictured on right)

3 whole chicken breasts,
   skinned, boned, halved
½ cup chopped onion
1 tablespoon oil
1 cup ketchup
½ cup firmly packed brown
   sugar
½ teaspoon grated orange peel
1½ cups fresh or frozen
   cranberries

Heat oven to 400°F. Grease 13x9-inch (3-quart) baking dish. Place chicken breast halves in greased dish. Bake at 400°F. for 25 minutes. Meanwhile, in medium skillet over medium heat, cook and stir onion in hot oil until crisp-tender. Add ketchup, brown sugar and orange peel; blend until brown sugar is dissolved. Stir in cranberries. Spoon over partially baked chicken breasts. Bake an additional 20 minutes or until chicken is tender. 6 servings.

NUTRITION INFORMATION PER SERVING

SERVING SIZE: 1/6 OF RECIPE		PERCENT U.S. RDA PER SERVING	
CALORIES	290	PROTEIN	40%
PROTEIN	28g	VITAMIN A	10%
CARBOHYDRATE	34g	VITAMIN C	10%
FAT	6g	THIAMINE	8%
CHOLESTEROL	73mg	RIBOFLAVIN	8%
SODIUM	610mg	NIACIN	60%
POTASSIUM	540mg	CALCIUM	4%
		IRON	10%

Pictured top to bottom: Chicken Cranberry Bake, Winter Green Salad p. 55

Strips of chicken and chunks of pineapple bake in a sweet-sour sauce.

PINEAPPLE CHICKEN

½ cup thinly sliced onion
⅓ cup sugar
¼ teaspoon garlic powder
1 cup ketchup
1 (20-oz.) can pineapple chunks, drained, reserving ¾ cup liquid
2 tablespoons lemon juice
2 tablespoons soy sauce
3 whole chicken breasts, skinned, boned, cut into 3x1-inch strips
¼ cup flour
2 tablespoons oil
1 tablespoon sesame seed
Hot cooked rice

Heat oven to 375°F. In medium saucepan, combine onion, sugar, garlic powder, ketchup, ¾ cup reserved pineapple liquid, lemon juice and soy sauce. Bring to a boil. Reduce heat; cover and simmer 15 minutes, stirring occasionally.

In plastic bag or shallow bowl, toss chicken strips with flour to coat. In large skillet over medium heat, cook chicken in hot oil 4 to 5 minutes or until lightly browned. Arrange cooked chicken and pineapple in ungreased 12x8-inch (2-quart) baking dish. Top with sauce; sprinkle with sesame seed.

Bake at 375°F. for 20 to 25 minutes or until chicken is hot and sauce is bubbly. Serve over hot cooked rice. 6 servings.

NUTRITION INFORMATION PER SERVING

SERVING SIZE: 1/6 OF RECIPE		PERCENT U.S. RDA PER SERVING	
CALORIES	620	PROTEIN	50%
PROTEIN	35g	VITAMIN A	10%
CARBOHYDRATE	99g	VITAMIN C	25%
FAT	9g	THIAMINE	40%
CHOLESTEROL	73mg	RIBOFLAVIN	10%
SODIUM	950mg	NIACIN	80%
POTASSIUM	720mg	CALCIUM	6%
		IRON	25%

Plan a party menu around this entree—it can be prepared the night before.

SWISS PARTY CHICKEN

3 whole chicken breasts, skinned, boned, halved
1 (4.5-oz.) jar Green Giant® Whole Mushrooms, drained
8 oz. (2 cups) shredded Swiss cheese
1 (10¾-oz.) can condensed cream of mushroom soup with ⅓ less salt
¼ cup dairy sour cream
¼ cup dry sherry or chicken broth
¼ cup grated Parmesan cheese

Heat oven to 350°F. Place chicken breasts in ungreased 12x8-inch (2-quart) baking dish; add mushrooms. Sprinkle with Swiss cheese. In small bowl, combine soup, sour cream and sherry; blend well. Pour over chicken.*

Bake at 350°F. for 50 minutes. Sprinkle with Parmesan cheese. Bake an additional 5 to 10 minutes or until chicken is tender and juices run clear. Place chicken on serving plate. Stir sauce if necessary to blend. Serve with chicken. 6 servings.

TIP: *To make ahead, prepare recipe to * Cover and refrigerate up to 24 hours. Uncover; bake as directed above.

NUTRITION INFORMATION PER SERVING

SERVING SIZE: 1/6 OF RECIPE		PERCENT U.S. RDA PER SERVING	
CALORIES	380	PROTEIN	60%
PROTEIN	41g	VITAMIN A	8%
CARBOHYDRATE	7g	VITAMIN C	*
FAT	20g	THIAMINE	6%
CHOLESTEROL	118mg	RIBOFLAVIN	20%
SODIUM	540mg	NIACIN	60%
POTASSIUM	340mg	CALCIUM	45%
		IRON	6%

*Contains less than 2% of the U.S. RDA of this nutrient.

On busy days when schedules are hectic, this family-style main dish is quick to make and tastes great.

TURKEY ROLLS AND RICE CASSEROLE

6 to 8 slices (1 lb.) uncooked
   turkey breast slices
6 to 8 strips (2x½x½-inch)
   Cheddar cheese (about 3 oz.)
1 cup uncooked instant rice
½ cup Green Giant® Frozen Sweet
   Peas (from 16-oz. pkg.)
½ cup water
½ cup dairy sour cream
¼ teaspoon salt
1 (2.8-oz.) can french fried
   onions
1 (10¾-oz.) can condensed
   cream of mushroom soup
1 (4-oz.) can Green Giant®
   Mushrooms Pieces and
   Stems, undrained
¼ cup slivered almonds, if
   desired

Heat oven to 350°F. Grease 8-inch (2-quart) square baking dish or 2-quart casserole. Place 1 strip of cheese on 1 end of each turkey breast slice; roll up. Place, seam side down, in greased baking dish.

In large bowl, combine rice, peas, water, sour cream, salt, ½ cup of the french fried onions, soup and mushrooms; blend well. Pour over turkey rolls; cover.

Bake at 350°F. for 50 to 55 minutes or until mixture is bubbly and turkey is tender. Uncover; sprinkle with remaining french fried onions and the almonds. Bake an additional 5 minutes or until onions are hot.
4 to 6 servings.

NUTRITION INFORMATION PER SERVING

SERVING SIZE: 1/6 OF RECIPE		PERCENT U.S. RDA PER SERVING	
CALORIES	410	PROTEIN	40%
PROTEIN	26g	VITAMIN A	6%
CARBOHYDRATE	26g	VITAMIN C	2%
FAT	23g	THIAMINE	10%
CHOLESTEROL	71mg	RIBOFLAVIN	15%
SODIUM	760mg	NIACIN	30%
POTASSIUM	350mg	CALCIUM	15%
		IRON	10%

Add a tossed salad and dinner is ready!

TEMPTING TUNA CASSEROLE

8 oz. (3½ cups) uncooked bow-
   tie pasta or wide egg noodles
½ cup chopped onion
½ cup chopped red or green bell
   pepper
2 tablespoons margarine or
   butter
3 tablespoons flour
¼ teaspoon salt
¼ teaspoon pepper
2 cups milk
1 cup water
1 chicken-flavor bouillon cube
   or 1 teaspoon chicken-flavor
   instant bouillon
¼ cup chopped green olives
2 (6½-oz.) cans tuna, drained
1 (4½-oz.) jar Green Giant®
   Sliced Mushrooms, drained
Potato chips, crushed

Heat oven to 350°F. Cook pasta to desired doneness as directed on package. Drain; rinse with hot water. Set aside.

Grease 2-quart casserole. In large saucepan, cook and stir onion and red pepper in margarine until tender. Stir in flour, salt and pepper; blend well. Cook until mixture is smooth and bubbly. Gradually add milk, water and bouillon cube; bring to a boil, stirring constantly. Stir in olives, tuna and mushrooms. In greased casserole, combine tuna mixture and cooked pasta; sprinkle with potato chips. Bake at 350°F. for 30 minutes or until hot and bubbly. 4 (1½-cup) servings.

NUTRITION INFORMATION PER SERVING

SERVING SIZE: 1-1/2 CUPS		PERCENT U.S. RDA PER SERVING	
CALORIES	370	PROTEIN	50%
PROTEIN	33g	VITAMIN A	25%
CARBOHYDRATE	32g	VITAMIN C	30%
FAT	11g	THIAMINE	20%
CHOLESTEROL	24mg	RIBOFLAVIN	25%
SODIUM	1140mg	NIACIN	60%
POTASSIUM	610mg	CALCIUM	20%
		IRON	25%

FRESH-FROM-THE-OVEN BAKED GOODS

Nothing says "home sweet home" like the aroma of just-baked breads, coffee cakes and sweet rolls.

To bring that can't-be-beat aroma of just-baked bread home to you, we've assembled an assortment of yeast and quick breads, muffins, coffee cakes and rolls perfect for any occasion from brunch to breakfast to a sit-down family dinner. Hot roll mix, refrigerated doughs and good old-fashioned yeast create a combination to fit your schedule, whether time is short or you have an afternoon to while away in the kitchen.

SWEET ROLL DOUGH

6 to 7 cups Pillsbury's BEST® All
    Purpose or Unbleached Flour
½ cup sugar
2 teaspoons salt
2 pkg. active dry yeast
1 cup water
1 cup milk
½ cup margarine or butter
1 egg

Lightly spoon flour into measuring cup; level off. In large bowl, combine 3 cups of the flour, sugar, salt and yeast; blend well. In small saucepan, heat water, milk and margarine until very warm (120 to 130°F.). Add warm liquid and egg to flour mixture. Blend at low speed until moistened; beat 3 minutes at medium speed. By hand, stir in an additional 2½ to 3 cups flour until dough pulls cleanly away from sides of bowl.

On floured surface, knead in ½ to 1 cup flour until dough is smooth and elastic, about 5 to 10 minutes.* Place dough in greased bowl; cover loosely with greased plastic wrap and cloth towel. Let rise in warm place (80 to 85°F.) until light and doubled in size, about 45 to 60 minutes.

Punch down dough several times to remove all air bubbles. Divide dough in half; shape into Orange Rolls and Kolachy (this page) as directed in recipe.

TIP: *To make dough a day ahead, prepare to *. Place dough in greased bowl; cover with greased plastic wrap and refrigerate overnight. (Dough will rise in refrigerator.) Punch down dough and shape into Orange Rolls and Kolachy.

HIGH ALTITUDE—Above 3500 Feet: No change.

COOK'S NOTE
BAKING WITH YEAST

The temperature of liquids to be used with active dry yeast is important to successful baking with yeast. A yeast or candy thermometer can ensure accurate liquid temperatures. When active dry yeast is combined with dry ingredients, a very warm liquid of 120 to 130°F. can be used. When active dry yeast is added to liquid, the temperature should be 110 to 120°F.

Yeast dough doesn't rise when the active dry yeast is outdated (look for the expiration date on the yeast package), when liquid temperatures are too hot or too cold to activate the yeast, or when excessive salt is added to the dough.

Yeast doughs need a warm place (80 to 85°F.) in which to proof or rise. The necessary warmth can be achieved by covering a bowl of dough loosely with a cloth towel and:

• Placing it on a wire rack over a pan of hot water in a draft-free place.

• Placing it on the top rack of an unheated oven and placing a pan of hot water on the rack below.

• Turning on the oven to 400°F. for 1 minute, then turning the oven off and placing the bowl on the center rack.

When the dough is doubled in size, a dent will remain in the dough when it is poked lightly with two fingers.

Pictured on previous page, left to right:
Orange Rolls, Kolachy

The home-baked flavor of these frosted orange rolls will be a hit at your next luncheon or shower. They're special but surprisingly easy!

ORANGE ROLLS

(pictured on p. 30)

½ **recipe Sweet Roll Dough (this page)**
2 **tablespoons margarine or butter, melted**
⅓ **cup sugar**
2 **teaspoons grated orange peel**

ORANGE FROSTING
½ **cup powdered sugar**
1 **tablespoon margarine or butter, softened**
1 **to 2 tablespoons orange juice**

Generously grease 18 muffin cups. On lightly floured surface, roll out dough to 18x12-inch rectangle. Spread with 2 tablespoons melted margarine. In small bowl, combine sugar and orange peel; blend well. Sprinkle over dough. Starting with 18-inch side, roll up. Pinch edges firmly to seal. Cut into eighteen 1-inch slices; place, cut side down, in greased muffin cups. Cover loosely with greased plastic wrap and cloth towel. Let rise in warm place (80 to 85°F.) until light and almost doubled in size, about 30 to 45 minutes.

Heat oven to 350°F. Uncover dough. Bake at 350°F. for 15 to 20 minutes or until golden brown. Immediately remove from muffin cups. In small bowl, combine frosting ingredients, adding enough orange juice for desired frosting consistency. Frost warm rolls. Serve warm. 18 rolls.

HIGH ALTITUDE—Above 3500 Feet: No change.

NUTRITION INFORMATION PER SERVING

SERVING SIZE: 1 ROLL		PERCENT U.S. RDA PER SERVING	
CALORIES	170	PROTEIN	4%
PROTEIN	3g	VITAMIN A	4%
CARBOHYDRATE	29g	VITAMIN C	*
FAT	5g	THIAMINE	15%
CHOLESTEROL	6mg	RIBOFLAVIN	8%
SODIUM	180mg	NIACIN	8%
POTASSIUM	50mg	CALCIUM	*
		IRON	6%

*Contains less than 2% of the U.S. RDA of this nutrient.

*One of our food editors shares a specialty her mother has made for many years. The name of this Bohemian bun, kolachy, comes from the word **kolac**, meaning round.*

KOLACHY

(pictured on p. 31)

½ **recipe Sweet Roll Dough (this page)**
½ **cup prepared prune or apricot filling**
2 **tablespoons margarine or butter, melted**
Sugar

Grease 2 large cookie sheets. On lightly floured surface, roll out dough to 18x12-inch rectangle. Cut into twenty-four 3-inch squares. Place 1 teaspoonful filling in center of each square. Gently pull opposite corners of square over filling. Repeat with other 2 corners, wrapping top corner around kolachy and tucking it under. Place 2 inches apart on greased cookie sheets. Cover loosely with greased plastic wrap and cloth towel. Let rise in warm place (80 to 85°F.) until light and almost doubled in size, about 30 to 45 minutes.

Heat oven to 350°F. Uncover dough. Bake at 350°F. for 15 to 20 minutes or until golden brown. Remove from pan. Brush with margarine; roll tops in sugar. Serve warm. 24 rolls.

HIGH ALTITUDE—Above 3500 Feet: No change.

NUTRITION INFORMATION PER SERVING

SERVING SIZE: 1 ROLL		PERCENT U.S. RDA PER SERVING	
CALORIES	120	PROTEIN	2%
PROTEIN	2g	VITAMIN A	2%
CARBOHYDRATE	20g	VITAMIN C	*
FAT	3g	THIAMINE	10%
CHOLESTEROL	5mg	RIBOFLAVIN	6%
SODIUM	130mg	NIACIN	6%
POTASSIUM	35mg	CALCIUM	*
		IRON	6%

*Contains less than 2% of the U.S. RDA of this nutrient.

Doughnuts were originally known as "nuts" of yeast dough. One type of doughnut, the bismarck, was named after a German statesman. It is traditionally filled with jelly or jam.

BISMARCKS

3 to 3½ cups Pillsbury's BEST®
   All Purpose or Unbleached
   Flour
¼ cup sugar
1½ teaspoons salt
1 teaspoon nutmeg
1 pkg. active dry yeast
½ cup water
½ cup milk
2 tablespoons shortening
1 egg
   Oil for deep frying
   Sugar
½ to ¾ cup raspberry preserves

Lightly spoon flour into measuring cup; level off. In large bowl, combine 1 cup of the flour, ¼ cup sugar, salt, nutmeg and yeast. In small saucepan, heat water, milk and shortening until very warm (120 to 130°F.). Add warm liquid and egg to flour mixture; beat until smooth. Stir in 2 to 2½ cups flour to form a stiff dough. Place in greased bowl. Cover; refrigerate 3 hours or overnight.

On floured surface, roll dough to ½-inch thickness. Cut with floured 2½-inch round cookie cutter. Place on large lightly floured cookie sheet. Cover loosely with cloth towel. Let rise in warm place (80 to 85°F.) until light and doubled in size, about 1 to 1½ hours.

In heavy saucepan or deep fryer, heat 2 to 3 inches oil to 375°F. Fry 2 to 3 circles of dough at a time until deep golden brown, 1 to 2 minutes on each side. Drain on paper towels. While warm, roll in sugar. With knife, cut 1-inch slit in side of each bismarck, cutting in toward center. Using small spoon, fill each slit with teaspoonful of the preserves.* Serve warm. 14 to 16 bismarcks.

TIP: *A decorating tube or cookie press with large writing tip can be used to fill bismarcks.

HIGH ALTITUDE—Above 3500 Feet: No change.

NUTRITION INFORMATION PER SERVING

SERVING SIZE: 1 BISMARCK		PERCENT U.S. RDA PER SERVING	
CALORIES	210	PROTEIN	6%
PROTEIN	4 g	VITAMIN A	*
CARBOHYDRATE	38 g	VITAMIN C	*
FAT	5 g	THIAMINE	15%
CHOLESTEROL	14 mg	RIBOFLAVIN	10%
SODIUM	210 mg	NIACIN	8%
POTASSIUM	65 mg	CALCIUM	*
		IRON	8%

*Contains less than 2% of the U.S. RDA of this nutrient.

VARIATION:
CUSTARD-TOPPED BISMARCKS: Substitute 2 (4-oz.) containers prepared vanilla pudding for preserves. Prepare dough as directed above. Just before frying, with thumb press 2-inch wide indentation in center of each circle. Fry, indented side down, 1 to 2 minutes; turn and fry 1 to 2 minutes on other side. Drain on paper towels, indented side down. Roll warm bismarcks in sugar. Just before serving, fill each indentation with heaping teaspoonful prepared vanilla pudding. Store in refrigerator.

Reminiscent of hot cross buns, these tender, delicious rum rolls are topped with a shiny rum glaze.

RUM BUNS

ROLLS
- 1 pkg. Pillsbury Hot Roll Mix
- 2 tablespoons sugar
- 1 cup water heated to 120 to 130°F.
- 2 tablespoons margarine or butter, softened
- 2 teaspoons rum extract
- ¼ cup raisins
- 1 egg

GLAZE
- 1 cup powdered sugar
- 2 tablespoons water
- 1 teaspoon rum extract

Grease large cookie sheet. In large bowl, combine flour mixture with yeast from foil packet and sugar; mix well. Stir in 1 cup **hot** water, margarine, 2 teaspoons rum extract, raisins and egg until dough pulls away from sides of bowl. Turn dough out onto lightly floured surface. With greased or floured hands, shape dough into a ball. Knead dough 5 minutes until smooth. Cover with large bowl. Let rest 5 minutes.

Divide dough into 12 pieces; shape into balls. Place 2 inches apart on greased cookie sheet. Cover loosely with greased plastic wrap and cloth towel. Let rise in warm place (80 to 85°F.) 20 to 30 minutes or until doubled in size.

Heat oven to 375°F. Uncover dough. Bake at 375°F. for 13 to 18 minutes or until golden brown. In small bowl, combine all glaze ingredients. Immediately brush or spoon glaze over warm rolls. Serve warm. 12 rolls.

HIGH ALTITUDE—Above 3500 Feet: No change.

COOK'S NOTE
FREEZING ROLLS
Tender and tasty homemade rolls add a special dimension to mealtimes. It is often more convenient to make and bake yeast rolls ahead and freeze them.

To freeze, cool the baked rolls completely. Place them on foil-wrapped cardboard before packaging in large plastic bags. Label the bags and freeze the rolls up to one month. For a fresh-baked flavor and texture, reheat rolls before serving them.

NUTRITION INFORMATION PER SERVING

SERVING SIZE: 1 ROLL		PERCENT U.S. RDA PER SERVING	
CALORIES	210	PROTEIN	8%
PROTEIN	5g	VITAMIN A	2%
CARBOHYDRATE	41g	VITAMIN C	*
FAT	3g	THIAMINE	15%
CHOLESTEROL	18mg	RIBOFLAVIN	15%
SODIUM	290mg	NIACIN	10%
POTASSIUM	80mg	CALCIUM	*
		IRON	8%

*Contains less than 2% of the U.S. RDA of this nutrient.

♥   ♥   ♥

Serve these as an early morning or mid-afternoon treat, or make a batch for a special friend.

GRAHAM NUT MUFFINS

(pictured on left)

1 cup graham cracker crumbs
   (about 12 crackers)
½ cup Pillsbury's BEST® All
   Purpose or Unbleached Flour
¼ cup whole wheat flour
½ cup firmly packed brown sugar
3 teaspoons baking powder
¼ cup chopped pecans, if desired
¼ cup chopped dates
3 egg whites
½ cup skim milk
¼ cup oil

Heat oven to 375°F. Line 12 muffin cups with paper baking cups or generously grease. Lightly spoon flour into measuring cup; level off. In large bowl, combine graham cracker crumbs, all purpose flour, whole wheat flour, brown sugar and baking powder; mix well. Stir in pecans and dates.

Slightly beat egg whites in small bowl. Add milk and oil; blend well. Add to dry ingredients all at once; stir until dry ingredients are just moistened. Fill lined or greased muffin cups ¾ full.

Bake at 375°F. for 16 to 19 minutes or until toothpick inserted in center comes out clean. Cool 1 minute; remove from pan. 12 muffins.

HIGH ALTITUDE—Above 3500 Feet: Increase all purpose flour to ¾ cup. Bake as directed above.

NUTRITION INFORMATION PER SERVING

SERVING SIZE: 1 MUFFIN		PERCENT U.S. RDA PER SERVING	
CALORIES	160	PROTEIN	4%
PROTEIN	3g	VITAMIN A	*
CARBOHYDRATE	24g	VITAMIN C	*
FAT	7g	THIAMINE	4%
CHOLESTEROL	0mg	RIBOFLAVIN	8%
SODIUM	140mg	NIACIN	4%
POTASSIUM	140mg	CALCIUM	6%
		IRON	6%

*Contains less than 2% of the U.S. RDA of this nutrient.

This recipe makes one and a half dozen muffins—some to enjoy warm and some to freeze for a later use.

BANANA CHOCOLATE CHIP MUFFINS

½ cup margarine or butter,
   softened
½ cup firmly packed brown
   sugar
1½ cups (3 large) mashed ripe
   bananas
¼ cup milk
1 teaspoon vanilla
2 eggs
2 cups Pillsbury's BEST® All
   Purpose or Unbleached
   Flour
1 teaspoon baking powder
1 teaspoon baking soda
¼ teaspoon salt
½ cup miniature chocolate
   chips
½ cup chopped walnuts

Heat oven to 375°F. Grease bottoms only of 18 muffin cups or line with paper baking cups. In large bowl, beat margarine and brown sugar until fluffy. Add bananas, milk, vanilla and eggs; blend well. Lightly spoon flour into measuring cup; level off. Add flour, baking powder, baking soda and salt; stir just until dry ingredients are moistened. Stir in chocolate chips and walnuts. Fill greased muffin cups ⅔ full.

Bake at 375°F. for 20 to 25 minutes or until toothpick inserted in center comes out clean. Cool 3 minutes before removing from pan. Serve warm. 18 muffins.

HIGH ALTITUDE—Above 3500 Feet: Decrease baking soda to ½ teaspoon. Bake at 400°F. for 20 to 25 minutes.

NUTRITION INFORMATION PER SERVING

SERVING SIZE: 1 MUFFIN		PERCENT U.S. RDA PER SERVING	
CALORIES	190	PROTEIN	4%
PROTEIN	3g	VITAMIN A	4%
CARBOHYDRATE	25g	VITAMIN C	2%
FAT	10g	THIAMINE	8%
CHOLESTEROL	24mg	RIBOFLAVIN	8%
SODIUM	180mg	NIACIN	4%
POTASSIUM	160mg	CALCIUM	2%
		IRON	6%

Graham Nut Muffins

*Here's a new twist to cinnamon
rolls, made easy with refrigerated
breadsticks. Children will love to
help twist and shape the dough.*

CINNAMON SUGAR
TWISTS

(pictured on right)

**8 (10 to 12-inch) wooden
chopsticks or metal skewers***
⅓ cup sugar
½ teaspoon cinnamon
**1 (11-oz.) can Pillsbury's
Refrigerated Soft Breadsticks**
**2 tablespoons margarine or
butter, melted**

Heat oven to 350°F. Grease
chopsticks. In small bowl, combine
sugar and cinnamon; sprinkle evenly
onto ungreased 15x10x1-inch baking
pan. Unroll dough; separate into
strips. Twist strip of dough around
each greased chopstick to within
½ inch of ends. Brush with margarine
to generously coat. Roll in cinnamon-
sugar mixture. Place on 1 large or
2 small ungreased cookie sheets,
tucking ends of dough under to
secure.

Bake at 350°F. for 10 to 20 minutes or
until golden brown. Immediately
remove from cookie sheet. Remove
chopsticks. Serve warm.** 8 rolls.

TIPS: *Wooden chopsticks can be found
in the oriental section of most
supermarkets.

**To reheat, wrap loosely in foil;
heat at 350°F. for 5 to 7 minutes
or until warm.

NUTRITION INFORMATION PER SERVING

SERVING SIZE: 1 ROLL		PERCENT U.S. RDA PER SERVING	
CALORIES	160	PROTEIN	4%
PROTEIN	3g	VITAMIN A	2%
CARBOHYDRATE	25g	VITAMIN C	*
FAT	5g	THIAMINE	100%
CHOLESTEROL	0mg	RIBOFLAVIN	6%
SODIUM	270mg	NIACIN	6%
POTASSIUM	25mg	CALCIUM	*
		IRON	6%

*Contains less than 2% of the U.S. RDA of this nutrient.

Cinnamon Sugar Twists

Here's a quicker version of the ever popular "elephant ears."

QUICK CRESCENT CINNAMON CRISPS

1 (8-oz.) can Pillsbury
   Refrigerated Quick Crescent
   Dinner Rolls
2 tablespoons margarine or
   butter, melted
⅓ cup sugar
1 teaspoon cinnamon
¼ cup finely chopped pecans

Heat oven to 375°F. Unroll dough into 2 long rectangles; firmly press perforations to seal. Brush with margarine. In small bowl, combine sugar and cinnamon; blend well. Sprinkle half of mixture over dough; sprinkle with pecans. Starting at shorter side, roll up each rectangle.

Cut each roll crosswise into 4 slices. On ungreased cookie sheet, pat or roll out each slice to a 4-inch circle; sprinkle each with remaining sugar-cinnamon mixture. Bake at 375°F. for 10 to 15 minutes or until golden brown. 8 rolls.

NUTRITION INFORMATION PER SERVING

SERVING SIZE: 1 ROLL		PERCENT U.S. RDA PER SERVING	
CALORIES	180	PROTEIN	2%
PROTEIN	2g	VITAMIN A	2%
CARBOHYDRATE	20g	VITAMIN C	*
FAT	11g	THIAMINE	6%
CHOLESTEROL	11mg	RIBOFLAVIN	2%
SODIUM	260mg	NIACIN	4%
POTASSIUM	80mg	CALCIUM	*
		IRON	4%

*Contains less than 2% of the U.S. RDA of this nutrient.

When you present a plate of these treats warm from the oven, everyone will applaud the baker!

CRESCENT ALMOND BEAR CLAWS

¾ cup ground almonds
2 tablespoons flour
1 tablespoon powdered sugar
1 tablespoon margarine or
   butter
½ teaspoon almond extract
1 egg, slightly beaten, reserving
   1 tablespoon for glaze
1 (8-oz.) can Pillsbury
   Refrigerated Quick Crescent
   Dinner Rolls
2 tablespoons sliced almonds
1 to 2 tablespoons sugar

In small bowl, combine ground almonds, flour, powdered sugar, margarine, almond extract and egg. Refrigerate mixture 15 minutes for easier handling, if necessary.

Heat oven to 375°F. Grease cookie sheet. Unroll dough into 2 long rectangles; firmly press perforations to seal. Roll half of almond filling into 13-inch rope; place lengthwise down center of 1 rectangle. Repeat with remaining filling and dough. Fold dough over almond filling, pressing unfolded edges to seal. Cut each strip crosswise into 4 pieces; place on greased cookie sheet. With sharp knife, cut 4 slashes in each piece from unfolded edge to center. Curve each piece slightly to fan out and form claw shape. Brush tops with reserved 1 tablespoon beaten egg; sprinkle with sliced almonds and sugar. Bake at 375°F. for 12 to 15 minutes or until golden brown. Serve warm. 8 rolls.

NUTRITION INFORMATION PER SERVING

SERVING SIZE: 1 ROLL		PERCENT U.S. RDA PER SERVING	
CALORIES	200	PROTEIN	6%
PROTEIN	5g	VITAMIN A	*
CARBOHYDRATE	19g	VITAMIN C	*
FAT	13g	THIAMINE	8%
CHOLESTEROL	30mg	RIBOFLAVIN	10%
SODIUM	260mg	NIACIN	6%
POTASSIUM	150mg	CALCIUM	2%
		IRON	6%

*Contains less than 2% of the U.S. RDA of this nutrient.

You will enjoy a country kitchen aroma as this yeast bread bakes.

HOT ROLL WHEAT BATTER BREAD

1 pkg. Pillsbury Hot Roll Mix
½ cup wheat germ
1¼ cups water heated to 120 to 130°F.
2 tablespoons molasses
2 tablespoons oil
1 egg

In large bowl, combine flour mixture with yeast from foil packet and wheat germ; mix well. Stir in **hot** water, molasses, oil and egg until well mixed (batter will be sticky). Cover bowl loosely with plastic wrap and cloth towel. Let rise in warm place (80 to 85°F.) 30 minutes.

Grease 2-quart casserole. Stir down dough; spread in greased casserole. Cover; let rise in warm place 30 minutes.

Heat oven to 375°F. Uncover dough. Bake at 375°F. for 30 to 35 minutes or until deep golden brown. Immediately remove from casserole. 1 (16-slice) loaf.

HIGH ALTITUDE—Above 3500 Feet: No change.

NUTRITION INFORMATION PER SERVING

SERVING SIZE: 1 SLICE		PERCENT U.S. RDA PER SERVING	
CALORIES	140	PROTEIN	6%
PROTEIN	5g	VITAMIN A	*
CARBOHYDRATE	24g	VITAMIN C	*
FAT	3g	THIAMINE	15%
CHOLESTEROL	13mg	RIBOFLAVIN	10%
SODIUM	200mg	NIACIN	10%
POTASSIUM	100mg	CALCIUM	*
		IRON	8%

*Contains less than 2% of the U.S. RDA of this nutrient.

Here's a nice accompaniment to a meal.

SPOON BREAD WITH CORN AND CHEESE

1 cup cornmeal
1 cup milk
1 (8.5-oz.) can Green Giant® Cream Style Golden Sweet Corn
½ cup margarine or butter
2 eggs
4 oz. (1 cup) shredded colby cheese
¼ cup chopped stuffed green olives, drained
¼ teaspoon dried dill weed

Heat oven to 375°F. Grease 1-quart casserole. In medium saucepan over medium heat, combine cornmeal, milk and corn; mix well. Bring to a boil, stirring constantly. Remove from heat; stir in margarine. Add eggs 1 at a time, beating by hand after each addition. Stir in cheese, olives and dill. Pour batter into greased casserole.

Bake at 375°F. for 30 to 35 minutes or until golden brown. Serve immediately topped with additional margarine or butter, if desired. Refrigerate leftovers. 4 (½-cup) servings.

HIGH ALTITUDE—Above 3500 Feet: No change.

NUTRITION INFORMATION PER SERVING

SERVING SIZE: 1/2 CUP		PERCENT U.S. RDA PER SERVING	
CALORIES	550	PROTEIN	25%
PROTEIN	15g	VITAMIN A	35%
CARBOHYDRATE	38g	VITAMIN C	2%
FAT	38g	THIAMINE	10%
CHOLESTEROL	138mg	RIBOFLAVIN	25%
SODIUM	880mg	NIACIN	8%
POTASSIUM	340mg	CALCIUM	30%
		IRON	10%

COOK'S NOTE
SPOON BREAD
Spoon bread is a custard-like cornbread that is baked in a casserole and served hot from the oven. It dates back to the 19th century in America when a recipe of cornbread with extra eggs and milk was forgotten in the oven. The result became known as spoon bread. It is served as a side dish, often in small bowls, and eaten with a spoon or fork.

Serve this bread warm with Bean and Bacon Combo (see Index). It's also great toasted!

HEARTY GRAIN QUICK LOAF

(pictured on p. 15)

2 cups Pillsbury's BEST® All Purpose or Unbleached Flour
1 cup Pillsbury's BEST® Whole Wheat Flour
½ cup quick-cooking rolled oats
¼ cup sugar
3 teaspoons baking powder
¾ teaspoon salt
1 egg
1½ cups milk
3 tablespoons oil
1 to 2 tablespoons quick-cooking rolled oats

Heat oven to 350°F. Grease bottom only of 8-inch round pan. Lightly spoon flour into measuring cup; level off. In large bowl, combine all purpose flour, whole wheat flour, ½ cup rolled oats, sugar, baking powder and salt; mix well.

Beat egg in small bowl. Add milk and oil; blend well. Add to dry ingredients all at once; stir until dry ingredients are just moistened. Spread dough in greased pan. Sprinkle with 1 to 2 tablespoons rolled oats.

Bake at 350°F. for 42 to 47 minutes or until golden brown and toothpick inserted in center comes out clean. Cool 5 minutes; remove from pan. Serve warm. 1 (16-slice) loaf.

HIGH ALTITUDE—Above 3500 Feet: Spread dough in greased 9-inch round pan. Bake as directed above.

NUTRITION INFORMATION PER SERVING

SERVING SIZE: 1 SLICE		PERCENT U.S. RDA PER SERVING	
CALORIES	150	PROTEIN	6%
PROTEIN	4g	VITAMIN A	*
CARBOHYDRATE	24g	VITAMIN C	*
FAT	4g	THIAMINE	10%
CHOLESTEROL	15mg	RIBOFLAVIN	8%
SODIUM	170mg	NIACIN	6%
POTASSIUM	100mg	CALCIUM	6%
		IRON	6%

*Contains less than 2% of the U.S. RDA of this nutrient.

COOK'S NOTE
WHOLE WHEAT FLOUR

Whole wheat flour is milled from the entire wheat kernel — endosperm, bran and germ. Baked products made with whole wheat flour have a heavier, more compact texture. Because the wheat germ contains fat, whole grain flour is susceptible to becoming rancid. It should be refrigerated or frozen in an airtight container if it is to be stored for a long period of time.

Cinnamon and ginger give a special flavor to this quick bread. The use of oil and egg whites results in a low fat, no cholesterol loaf.

WHOLE WHEAT PEAR QUICK BREAD

1¼ cups Pillsbury's BEST® All Purpose or Unbleached Flour
½ cup Pillsbury's BEST® Whole Wheat Flour
¾ cup sugar
1 teaspoon baking soda
½ teaspoon salt
½ teaspoon cinnamon
¼ teaspoon ginger
¼ cup oil
2 egg whites
1 (8.50-oz.) can lite pear halves, drained, chopped, reserving ¼ cup liquid
¼ cup coarsely chopped pecans, if desired

Heat oven to 325°F. Grease and flour bottom only of 8x4-inch loaf pan. Lightly spoon flour into measuring cup; level off. In large bowl, combine all purpose flour, whole wheat flour, sugar, baking soda, salt, cinnamon, ginger, oil, egg whites, pears and reserved ¼ cup pear liquid. Blend at low speed until moistened; beat 3 minutes at medium speed. Stir in pecans. Pour batter into greased and floured pan.

Bake at 325°F. for 65 to 75 minutes or until toothpick inserted in center comes out clean. Cool 5 minutes; remove from pan. Cool on wire rack. 1 (16-slice) loaf.

HIGH ALTITUDE—Above 3500 Feet: Bake at 350°F. for 53 to 58 minutes.

NUTRITION INFORMATION PER SERVING

SERVING SIZE: 1 SLICE		PERCENT U.S. RDA PER SERVING	
CALORIES	140	PROTEIN	2%
PROTEIN	2g	VITAMIN A	*
CARBOHYDRATE	22g	VITAMIN C	*
FAT	5g	THIAMINE	6%
CHOLESTEROL	0mg	RIBOFLAVIN	4%
SODIUM	140mg	NIACIN	4%
POTASSIUM	50mg	CALCIUM	*
		IRON	4%

*Contains less than 2% of the U.S. RDA of this nutrient.

This is truly an early morning delight. Invite a friend and serve it with coffee or tea.

OVERNIGHT COFFEE CAKE SWIRL

CAKE
1 cup Pillsbury's BEST® All Purpose Flour or Unbleached Flour
¼ cup sugar
¼ cup firmly packed brown sugar
1 teaspoon baking powder
½ teaspoon baking soda
¼ teaspoon salt
½ cup buttermilk*
⅓ cup shortening
1 egg

TOPPING
¼ cup firmly packed brown sugar
¼ cup chopped nuts
¼ teaspoon nutmeg

Grease and flour 9-inch round or 8-inch square pan. In small bowl, combine all cake ingredients. Blend at low speed until moistened; beat 2 minutes at medium speed. Pour batter into greased and floured pan. In small bowl, combine all topping ingredients; blend well. Sprinkle over batter. Cover; refrigerate overnight.

Heat oven to 350°F. Uncover coffee cake. Bake at 350°F. for 25 to 35 minutes or until toothpick inserted in center comes out clean. Serve warm. 8 servings.

TIP: *To substitute for buttermilk, use 1½ teaspoons vinegar or lemon juice plus milk to make ½ cup.

HIGH ALTITUDE—Above 3500 Feet: No change.

NUTRITION INFORMATION PER SERVING

SERVING SIZE: 1/8 OF RECIPE		PERCENT U.S. RDA PER SERVING	
CALORIES	250	PROTEIN	4%
PROTEIN	3g	VITAMIN A	*
CARBOHYDRATE	33g	VITAMIN C	*
FAT	12g	THIAMINE	10%
CHOLESTEROL	27mg	RIBOFLAVIN	8%
SODIUM	200mg	NIACIN	4%
POTASSIUM	115mg	CALCIUM	6%
		IRON	8%

*Contains less than 2% of the U.S. RDA of this nutrient.

This moist coffee cake, flavored with lemon and swirled with raspberry preserves, is perfect for a Valentine's Day brunch.

MARBLED RASPBERRY COFFEE CAKE

(pictured on left)

COFFEE CAKE
- 1 cup Pillsbury's BEST® All Purpose or Unbleached Flour
- ½ cup sugar
- 1 teaspoon baking powder
- ¼ teaspoon baking soda
- ¼ teaspoon salt
- 1 (3-oz.) pkg. cream cheese, softened
- ¼ cup margarine or butter, softened
- ¼ cup milk
- 1 teaspoon grated lemon peel
- 1 egg
- ¼ cup raspberry preserves

FROSTING
- ½ cup powdered sugar
- 1 tablespoon lemon juice
- 2 teaspoons margarine or butter, softened
- ¼ cup sliced almonds

Heat oven to 350°F. Grease and flour 8-inch square pan. Lightly spoon flour into measuring cup; level off. In small bowl, combine flour and remaining coffee cake ingredients except preserves; blend at low speed until moistened. Beat 2 minutes at medium speed. Spread batter into greased and floured pan. Spoon preserves by teaspoonfuls over batter. Using knife, swirl preserves over top of batter to marble.

Bake at 350°F. for 25 to 30 minutes or until toothpick inserted in center comes out clean. Cool slightly.

In small bowl, combine all frosting ingredients except almonds; beat until smooth. Frost warm cake; sprinkle with almonds. Serve warm. 9 servings.

HIGH ALTITUDE—Above 3500 Feet: No change.

NUTRITION INFORMATION PER SERVING

SERVING SIZE: 1/9 OF RECIPE		PERCENT U.S. RDA PER SERVING	
CALORIES	250	PROTEIN	6%
PROTEIN	4g	VITAMIN A	8%
CARBOHYDRATE	34g	VITAMIN C	*
FAT	11g	THIAMINE	8%
CHOLESTEROL	34mg	RIBOFLAVIN	8%
SODIUM	230mg	NIACIN	4%
POTASSIUM	75mg	CALCIUM	4%
		IRON	6%

*Contains less than 2% of the U.S. RDA of this nutrient.

COOK'S NOTE
MEASURING FLOUR

Most flour on the market today is presifted. To measure flour, stir it, then spoon it lightly into a standard dry measuring cup. Tap the cup gently to avoid air pockets and level it off with a straight-edged spatula or knife.

Marbled Raspberry Coffee Cake

Here is a treat for almond lovers. It combines old-fashioned goodness with the convenience of hot roll mix.

ALMOND YEAST COFFEE CAKE

(pictured on right)

1 pkg. Pillsbury Hot Roll Mix
2 tablespoons sugar
1 cup water heated to 120 to
    130°F.
2 tablespoons margarine or
    butter, softened
1 egg

FILLING

1 cup ground blanched almonds
2 tablespoons powdered sugar
1 tablespoon light corn syrup
1 tablespoon margarine or
    butter, melted
½ teaspoon almond extract
1 egg white

GLAZE

1 cup powdered sugar
1 to 2 tablespoons milk
¼ teaspoon almond extract

Grease 1 large or 2 small cookie sheets. In large bowl, combine flour mixture with yeast from foil packet and 2 tablespoons sugar; mix well. Stir in **hot** water, 2 tablespoons margarine and egg until dough pulls away from sides of bowl. Turn dough out onto lightly floured surface. With greased or floured hands, shape dough into a ball. Knead dough for 5 minutes until smooth. Cover with large bowl; let rest 5 minutes.

In small bowl, combine all filling ingredients; mix well. Set aside. On lightly floured surface, roll dough to a 16x10-inch rectangle. Spread filling evenly over dough. Starting with 16-inch side, roll up tightly. Cut lengthwise through center of roll, forming two 16-inch strips. Place 1 strip, cut side up, on greased cookie sheet. Form heart shape, with deep indentation at top of heart, sealing ends of dough at bottom of heart.

With scissors, clip top surface of hear at 1-inch intervals. Repeat shaping with remaining strip of dough. Cover loosely with greased plastic wrap and cloth towel. Let rise in warm place (80 to 85°F.) 20 to 30 minutes or until doubled in size.

Heat oven to 375°F. Uncover dough. Bake at 375°F. for 18 to 28 minutes or until golden brown. Cover with foil during last 10 to 15 minutes of baking if necessary to prevent excessive browning. Cool. In small bowl, combine all glaze ingredients, adding enough milk for desired glaze

consistency. Blend until smooth.
Drizzle over cooled coffee cakes.
Garnish with sliced almonds,
if desired.
2 coffee cakes; 8 servings each.

HIGH ALTITUDE—Above 3500 Feet:
No change.

Almond Yeast Coffee Cake

NUTRITION INFORMATION PER SERVING

SERVING SIZE: 1/16 OF RECIPE		PERCENT U.S. RDA PER SERVING	
CALORIES	200	PROTEIN	8%
PROTEIN	5g	VITAMIN A	2%
CARBOHYDRATE	32g	VITAMIN C	*
FAT	6g	THIAMINE	10%
CHOLESTEROL	13mg	RIBOFLAVIN	10%
SODIUM	230mg	NIACIN	8%
POTASSIUM	95mg	CALCIUM	2%
		IRON	6%

*Contains less than 2% of the U.S. RDA of this nutrient.

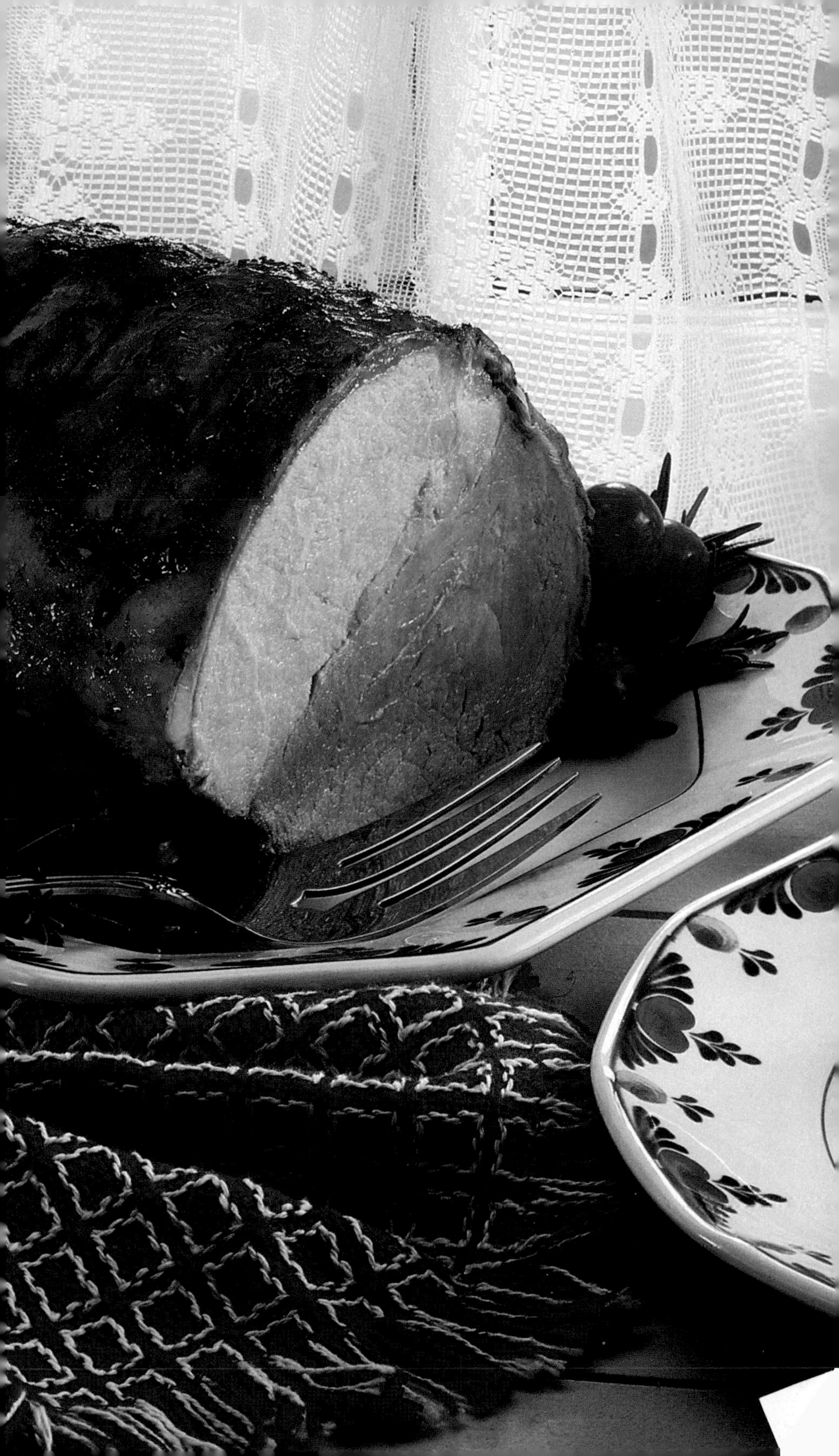

ALL-AMERICAN ACCOMPANIMENTS

These side dishes and salads round out meals from hot dogs to baked ham.

"A roast is just a roast" until you team it up with **Scalloped New Potatoes** and **Winter Green Salad,** and then it's a feast! These are two of the tempting side dishes and salads included in this chapter. These all-American accompaniments have been seasoned just so to complement meats and main dishes with a cornucopia of contemporary flavors from spicy to tangy, mellow to savory. And despite their home-cooked heritage, they're surprisingly simple to make.

Serve this full-flavored side dish with Herb-Marinated Roast (see Index) or poultry. It is important to cut the vegetables as directed in the recipe so they all bake in the same time.

WINTER VEGETABLES WITH ROSEMARY

(pictured on p. 49)

2 medium turnips or potatoes, peeled, cut into 1-inch pieces
2 medium parsnips, peeled, cut into 1-inch pieces
2 medium carrots, peeled, cut into ½-inch pieces
¼ cup olive oil
1 tablespoon finely chopped fresh rosemary or 2 teaspoons dried rosemary leaves
½ teaspoon salt
¼ teaspoon pepper
2 garlic cloves, minced
1 fennel bulb, cut into 1-inch pieces

Heat oven to 350°F.* Place turnips, parsnips and carrots in ungreased 12x8-inch (2-quart) baking dish. In small bowl, combine oil, rosemary, salt, pepper and garlic; blend well. Pour over vegetables; toss to coat. Cover; bake at 350°F. for 30 minutes. Stir in fennel. Bake uncovered an additional 1 to 1½ hours or until vegetables are tender, stirring occasionally. If desired, season with additional salt and pepper. 9 (½-cup) servings.

TIP: *This recipe can be baked at the same oven temperature as Herb-Marinated Roast.

NUTRITION INFORMATION PER SERVING

SERVING SIZE: 1/2 CUP		PERCENT U.S. RDA PER SERVING	
CALORIES	90	PROTEIN	*
PROTEIN	1 g	VITAMIN A	90%
CARBOHYDRATE	8 g	VITAMIN C	15%
FAT	6 g	THIAMINE	2%
CHOLESTEROL	0 mg	RIBOFLAVIN	*
SODIUM	160 mg	NIACIN	2%
POTASSIUM	250 mg	CALCIUM	2%
		IRON	2%

*Contains less than 2% of the U.S. RDA of this nutrient.

Pictured on previous page, left to right: Herb-Marinated Roast p. 20, Winter Vegetables with Rosemary

This is a great salad for a luncheon.

CREAMY WALDORF SALAD

4 cups (4 medium) apples, cubed
⅓ cup chopped celery
¼ cup maraschino cherries, drained, halved
¼ cup chopped pecans or walnuts
2 tablespoons raisins
⅓ cup vanilla yogurt
⅓ cup mayonnaise
⅓ cup whipping cream, whipped

In large bowl, combine all ingredients except whipped cream; mix well. Gently fold in whipped cream. Cover; refrigerate. 10 (½ cup) servings.

NUTRITION INFORMATION PER SERVING

SERVING SIZE: 1/2 CUP		PERCENT U.S. RDA PER SERVING	
CALORIES	140	PROTEIN	*
PROTEIN	1 g	VITAMIN A	2%
CARBOHYDRATE	12 g	VITAMIN C	4%
FAT	11 g	THIAMINE	*
CHOLESTEROL	16 mg	RIBOFLAVIN	2%
SODIUM	55 mg	NIACIN	*
POTASSIUM	115 mg	CALCIUM	2%
		IRON	*

*Contains less than 2% of the U.S. RDA of this nutrient.

COOK'S NOTE
TURNIPS AND PARSNIPS

Turnips and parsnips are root vegetables that contain a fair amount of vitamin C. Turnips have a white skin with a purple-tinged top. Parsnips are white and tapered like carrots. While somewhat strong tasting, both vegetables are sweet and rich in flavor.

To prepare, wash, trim and peel them. Turnips are good mashed, stir-fried, cubed and tossed with butter or used raw in salads. Parsnips are suitable for almost any method of cooking but are often boiled and mashed like potatoes.

Rice is sometimes called "the food of ages" for it is as old as history and rivals wheat as the world's most important food. This colorful side dish is a wonderful addition to a buffet table.

VEGETABLE CONFETTI RICE

2 cups water
1 tablespoon margarine or butter
1 chicken-flavor bouillon cube or 1 teaspoon chicken-flavor instant bouillon
¾ cup uncooked regular long grain rice
½ cup coarsely shredded carrot
½ cup sliced celery
1 tablespoon finely chopped onion
⅓ cup Green Giant® Harvest Fresh® Frozen Sweet Peas, thawed (from 16-oz. pkg.)

In medium saucepan, bring water, margarine and bouillon cube to a boil. Stir to dissolve bouillon cube. Add rice, carrot, celery and onion; mix well. Bring to a boil; reduce heat. Cover; simmer 20 minutes or until rice is tender and liquid is absorbed. Stir in peas; cook an additional 5 minutes. 6 (½-cup) servings.

NUTRITION INFORMATION PER SERVING

SERVING SIZE: 1/2 CUP		PERCENT U.S. RDA PER SERVING	
CALORIES	120	PROTEIN	4%
PROTEIN	3g	VITAMIN A	50%
CARBOHYDRATE	22g	VITAMIN C	4%
FAT	2g	THIAMINE	10%
CHOLESTEROL	0mg	RIBOFLAVIN	*
SODIUM	240mg	NIACIN	6%
POTASSIUM	110mg	CALCIUM	*
		IRON	6%

*Contains less than 2% of the U.S. RDA of this nutrient.

We like it hot! Great to serve with chicken or fish, this zesty side dish teams green chiles with whole grains.

BROWN RICE WITH CHILES

¾ cup chopped onions
½ cup chopped celery
2 tablespoons oil
¾ cup uncooked brown rice
¼ cup bulgur
1 (14½-oz.) can chicken broth
¾ cup water
2 tablespoons chopped fresh parsley or 2 teaspoons dried parsley flakes
2 teaspoons dried basil leaves
¼ teaspoon salt, if desired
1 (4-oz.) can diced green chiles, drained

Heat oven to 350°F. In large skillet over medium heat, cook onion and celery in hot oil until crisp-tender. Add brown rice and bulgur, stirring until lightly browned. Stir in remaining ingredients. Spoon into ungreased 1½-quart casserole. Cover; bake at 350°F. for 1¼ to 1½ hours or until rice is tender and liquid is absorbed. 8 (½-cup) servings.

NUTRITION INFORMATION PER SERVING

SERVING SIZE: 1/2 CUP		PERCENT U.S. RDA PER SERVING	
CALORIES	130	PROTEIN	4%
PROTEIN	3g	VITAMIN A	25%
CARBOHYDRATE	20g	VITAMIN C	35%
FAT	4g	THIAMINE	6%
CHOLESTEROL	0mg	RIBOFLAVIN	2%
SODIUM	240mg	NIACIN	10%
POTASSIUM	200mg	CALCIUM	2%
		IRON	4%

Pictured left to right: Coleslaw with Pasta, Vegetable Barley Salad

For a zippier cajun-style salad, add the cayenne pepper.

COLESLAW WITH PASTA

(pictured above)

SALAD
1 (16-oz.) pkg. Green Giant® Garden Herb Seasoning Pasta Accents® Frozen Vegetables with Pasta
2 cups coleslaw mix*

DRESSING
½ cup salad dressing or mayonnaise
1 teaspoon lemon juice
¼ teaspoon sugar
¼ teaspoon paprika
¼ teaspoon salt
⅛ teaspoon garlic powder
Dash to ⅛ teaspoon cayenne pepper, if desired

Prepare frozen vegetables with pasta as directed on package until vegetables are crisp-tender. Cover; refrigerate 1 hour.

Add coleslaw mix to chilled vegetables and pasta; toss gently. In small bowl, combine all dressing ingredients; blend well. Add to salad; toss gently to coat. Cover; refrigerate until ready to serve.
11 (½-cup) servings.

TIP: *Coleslaw mix is prepackaged shredded cabbage and carrots. It is available in the produce section of your supermarket.

NUTRITION INFORMATION PER SERVING

SERVING SIZE: 1/2 CUP		PERCENT U.S. RDA PER SERVING	
CALORIES	110	PROTEIN	2%
PROTEIN	2g	VITAMIN A	80%
CARBOHYDRATE	11g	VITAMIN C	20%
FAT	6g	THIAMINE	4%
CHOLESTEROL	8mg	RIBOFLAVIN	2%
SODIUM	280mg	NIACIN	2%
POTASSIUM	125mg	CALCIUM	2%
		IRON	2%

Serve this crunchy, flavorful salad warm or cold.

VEGETABLE BARLEY SALAD

(pictured above)

SALAD
- 1 (14½-oz.) can chicken broth
- ½ cup uncooked barley
- ¾ cup thinly sliced celery
- ½ cup sliced water chestnuts, drained
- ½ cup chopped green bell pepper
- ⅓ cup shredded carrot
- ¼ cup sliced green onions
- 1 tablespoon dried parsley flakes
- 1½ teaspoons dried dill weed
- ½ teaspoon dried basil leaves
- 1 (2.5-oz.) jar Green Giant® Sliced Mushrooms, drained

DRESSING
- 3 tablespoons olive oil or oil
- 2 tablespoons red wine vinegar
- ¼ teaspoon salt, if desired
- 1 garlic clove, minced

Bring chicken broth to a boil in medium saucepan. Stir in barley; reduce heat. Cover; simmer 40 to 45 minutes or until barley is tender. Drain, if necessary.

In large bowl, combine cooked barley and remaining salad ingredients; blend well. In small bowl using wire whisk, blend all dressing ingredients. Pour over salad; blend well. Serve warm or cold. 8 (½-cup) servings.

TIP: Leftover water chestnuts can be frozen for a later use.

NUTRITION INFORMATION PER SERVING

SERVING SIZE: 1/2 CUP		PERCENT U.S. RDA PER SERVING	
CALORIES	120	PROTEIN	4%
PROTEIN	3g	VITAMIN A	30%
CARBOHYDRATE	14g	VITAMIN C	10%
FAT	6g	THIAMINE	2%
CHOLESTEROL	0mg	RIBOFLAVIN	4%
SODIUM	310mg	NIACIN	8%
POTASSIUM	230mg	CALCIUM	2%
		IRON	4%

The combination of olives and cherries may seem unlikely, but a taste treat awaits you.

TROPICAL MOLDED SALAD

1 (20-oz.) can crushed
    pineapple, drained,
    reserving liquid
1 (3-oz.) pkg. lemon gelatin
¾ cup sugar
¼ cup lemon juice
1 teaspoon grated lemon peel
1 cup whipping cream
1 (3-oz.) pkg. cream cheese,
    softened
½ cup maraschino cherries,
    drained, chopped
½ cup green pimiento-stuffed
    olives, drained, sliced
⅓ cup chopped pecans

If necessary, add water to reserved pineapple liquid to make 1 cup. Prepare gelatin according to package directions, using pineapple liquid for the cold water. Refrigerate until slightly thickened, about 45 to 55 minutes. In medium saucepan, combine pineapple, sugar and lemon juice; blend well. Bring to a boil; boil 6 minutes, stirring occasionally. Add lemon peel; cool.

In small bowl, beat whipping cream until soft peaks form. In medium bowl, beat cream cheese until smooth. Add whipped cream; blend well. Stir into gelatin mixture. Fold in cool pineapple mixture, cherries, olives and pecans. Pour into 6-cup mold. Refrigerate 3 to 4 hours or until firm. Unmold; garnish as desired. 12 (½-cup) servings.

NUTRITION INFORMATION PER SERVING

SERVING SIZE: 1/2 CUP		PERCENT U.S. RDA PER SERVING	
CALORIES	240	PROTEIN	2%
PROTEIN	2g	VITAMIN A	8%
CARBOHYDRATE	30g	VITAMIN C	6%
FAT	13g	THIAMINE	4%
CHOLESTEROL	35mg	RIBOFLAVIN	2%
SODIUM	190mg	NIACIN	*
POTASSIUM	115mg	CALCIUM	2%
		IRON	2%

*Contains less than 2% of the U.S. RDA of this nutrient.

To save time, we've updated old-fashioned overnight fruit salad by using creamy yogurt for the cooked custard in the dressing.

OVERNIGHT FRUIT 'N' CREAM SALAD

CREAMY LEMON DRESSING
1 cup whipping cream
1 tablespoon sugar
1 (6-oz.) carton custard-style
    lemon yogurt

SALAD
2 cups miniature marshmallows
1 cup seedless green grapes
1 cup (1 medium) cubed apple
1 (16-oz.) can sliced peaches, well
    drained
2 firm bananas, sliced

In small bowl, beat whipping cream and sugar until stiff peaks form. Fold in yogurt; blend well. In large bowl, combine marshmallows, grapes, apple and peaches. Add dressing to fruit mixture; mix gently. Cover; refrigerate 8 hours or overnight. Just before serving, fold in bananas. Garnish if desired. 17 (½-cup) servings.

NUTRITION INFORMATION PER SERVING

SERVING SIZE: 1/2 CUP		PERCENT U.S. RDA PER SERVING	
CALORIES	110	PROTEIN	*
PROTEIN	1g	VITAMIN A	6%
CARBOHYDRATE	15g	VITAMIN C	6%
FAT	6g	THIAMINE	*
CHOLESTEROL	20mg	RIBOFLAVIN	2%
SODIUM	15mg	NIACIN	*
POTASSIUM	135mg	CALCIUM	*
		IRON	*

*Contains less than 2% of the U.S. RDA of this nutrient.

In this salad, the crunch of sugared pecans combines with the fruit for a pleasing taste and texture combination.

WINTER GREEN SALAD

(pictured on p. 27)

SALAD
¼ cup chopped pecans
2 tablespoons sugar
8 cups torn assorted greens
    (iceberg lettuce, spinach,
    romaine and/or Bibb lettuce)
2 cups sliced celery
2 cups green grapes, cut in half
    lengthwise
⅓ cup pomegranate seeds*
3 kiwifruit, peeled, sliced

DRESSING
¼ cup oil
2 tablespoons vinegar
2 tablespoons sugar
½ teaspoon salt

In small skillet, combine pecans and 2 tablespoons sugar. Stir over low heat until sugar melts and coats pecans. Remove from heat; spread pecans on waxed paper or foil. Cool; break up any clumps.

In large bowl, combine greens, celery, grapes, pomegranate seeds and kiwifruit. In small bowl using wire whisk, blend all dressing ingredients. Pour over salad mixture; add pecans. Toss gently. Serve immediately.
10 (1-cup) servings.

TIP: *One cup fresh raspberries can be substituted for pomegranate seeds. Add to salad mixture with pecans.

NUTRITION INFORMATION PER SERVING

SERVING SIZE: 1 CUP		PERCENT U.S. RDA PER SERVING	
CALORIES	140	PROTEIN	2%
PROTEIN	2g	VITAMIN A	25%
CARBOHYDRATE	18g	VITAMIN C	60%
FAT	8g	THIAMINE	6%
CHOLESTEROL	0mg	RIBOFLAVIN	4%
SODIUM	140mg	NIACIN	2%
POTASSIUM	370mg	CALCIUM	4%
		IRON	4%

This side dish is a creamier version of the traditional tart and tangy German Potato Salad.

CREAMY GERMAN POTATO SALAD

4 slices bacon
½ cup chopped onion
⅓ cup sugar
2 tablespoons flour
½ teaspoon salt
½ teaspoon celery seed
½ cup water
⅓ cup vinegar
2 lb. (5 cups) new red potatoes,
    cooked, peeled, sliced
½ cup dairy sour cream
    Fresh parsley, if desired

Cook bacon in large skillet over medium heat until crisp. Remove bacon; drain on paper towels. Crumble bacon; set aside.

Cook onion in bacon drippings until crisp-tender. Stir in sugar, flour, salt and celery seed; blend well. Cook until mixture is smooth and bubbly, stirring constantly. Gradually add water and vinegar. Cook until mixture boils and thickens, stirring constantly. Add potatoes and bacon; mix gently. Bring to a boil. Reduce heat; cover and simmer over low heat for 25 to 30 minutes to blend flavors. Gently stir in sour cream; cook until thoroughly heated. Garnish with fresh parsley. Serve hot. Store any remaining salad in refrigerator.
11 (½-cup) servings.

NUTRITION INFORMATION PER SERVING

SERVING SIZE: 1/2 CUP		PERCENT U.S. RDA PER SERVING	
CALORIES	120	PROTEIN	2%
PROTEIN	2g	VITAMIN A	2%
CARBOHYDRATE	20g	VITAMIN C	6%
FAT	4g	THIAMINE	6%
CHOLESTEROL	7mg	RIBOFLAVIN	2%
SODIUM	140mg	NIACIN	4%
POTASSIUM	230mg	CALCIUM	2%
		IRON	2%

With no added fat, this colorful side dish is a healthy, delicious choice. Serve it with Roast Pork Loin with Savory Stuffing (see Index).

DILLED CARROTS

(pictured on left)

¾ cup chicken broth
1 lb. carrots, cut into 2x¼-inch strips
1 cup sliced celery (½ inch thick)
2 tablespoons sliced green onions
2 tablespoons sugar
¾ teaspoon dried dill weed
1 (8-oz.) can sliced water chestnuts, drained
1 tablespoon chopped fresh parsley or 1 teaspoon dried parsley flakes

Bring broth to a boil in large saucepan. Add remaining ingredients except parsley. Cover; reduce heat to medium. Cook 10 to 15 minutes or until carrots are crisp-tender, stirring occasionally. Drain. Sprinkle with parsley. 8 (½-cup) servings.

NUTRITION INFORMATION PER SERVING

SERVING SIZE: 1/2 CUP		PERCENT U.S. RDA PER SERVING	
CALORIES	60	PROTEIN	2%
PROTEIN	1g	VITAMIN A	260%
CARBOHYDRATE	13g	VITAMIN C	8%
FAT	0g	THIAMINE	4%
CHOLESTEROL	0mg	RIBOFLAVIN	4%
SODIUM	105mg	NIACIN	4%
POTASSIUM	330mg	CALCIUM	2%
		IRON	2%

Here's a quick stovetop side dish enhanced with the flavors of bacon and a hint of mustard and paprika.

SAVORY SCALLOPED CORN

2 slices bacon
½ cup sliced green onions
1 tablespoon flour
½ teaspoon salt
¼ teaspoon dry mustard
¼ teaspoon paprika
⅛ teaspoon pepper
1 egg
1 cup milk
1 (16-oz.) pkg. Green Giant® Frozen Shoe Peg White Corn, thawed, drained*

Cook bacon in large skillet over medium heat until crisp. Remove bacon; drain on paper towel. Crumble bacon; set aside.

Cook green onions in bacon drippings until tender. Stir in flour, salt, dry mustard, paprika and pepper; blend well. Cook until mixture is smooth and bubbly, stirring constantly. Beat egg in small bowl; stir in milk. Gradually add to flour mixture; cook until mixture thickens, stirring constantly. Stir in corn. Cook until thoroughly heated. Sprinkle with bacon. 6 (½-cup) servings.

TIP: *One (16-oz.) pkg. Green Giant® Niblets® Frozen Corn can be substituted.

NUTRITION INFORMATION PER SERVING

SERVING SIZE: 1/2 CUP		PERCENT U.S. RDA PER SERVING	
CALORIES	120	PROTEIN	8%
PROTEIN	5g	VITAMIN A	4%
CARBOHYDRATE	20g	VITAMIN C	8%
FAT	3g	THIAMINE	6%
CHOLESTEROL	40mg	RIBOFLAVIN	10%
SODIUM	250mg	NIACIN	6%
POTASSIUM	270mg	CALCIUM	6%
		IRON	2%

Dilled Carrots

Baby vegetables are "in" and the oldest baby of all is the new potato. Try these tiny potatoes in this easy rendition of old-time scalloped potatoes.

SCALLOPED NEW POTATOES

(pictured on left)

1½ lb. new red potatoes,
    scrubbed, quartered
1 cup sliced onions
1 (10¾-oz.) can condensed
    cream of mushroom soup
    with ⅓ less salt
½ cup milk
2 tablespoons chopped fresh
    chives or 2 teaspoons
    freeze-dried chives
½ teaspoon dried dill weed
½ teaspoon dried marjoram
    Dash pepper

Arrange potatoes and onions in ungreased 8-inch square baking dish or 2-quart casserole. In medium bowl, combine remaining ingredients; blend well. Pour over potatoes and onions; cover. Bake at 350°F. for 1 hour. Uncover; bake an additional 15 to 30 minutes or until potatoes are tender. 10 (½-cup) servings.

🖾 MICROWAVE DIRECTIONS: Arrange potatoes and onions in 2-quart microwave-safe casserole. In medium bowl, combine remaining ingredients; blend well. Pour over potatoes and onions; cover. Microwave on HIGH for 15 to 18 minutes or until potatoes are tender, stirring twice during cooking. Let stand 5 minutes.

NUTRITION INFORMATION PER SERVING

SERVING SIZE: 1/2 CUP		PERCENT U.S. RDA PER SERVING	
CALORIES	110	PROTEIN	4%
PROTEIN	3g	VITAMIN A	*
CARBOHYDRATE	21g	VITAMIN C	10%
FAT	2g	THIAMINE	6%
CHOLESTEROL	2mg	RIBOFLAVIN	4%
SODIUM	160mg	NIACIN	6%
POTASSIUM	350mg	CALCIUM	2%
		IRON	6%

*Contains less than 2% of the U.S. RDA of this nutrient.

Scalloped New Potatoes

A nice blend of cheeses combine in this easily assembled side dish.

PARMESAN SWISS POTATOES

⅓ cup grated Parmesan cheese
1 tablespoon dried parsley flakes
2 tablespoons margarine or
   butter
2 tablespoons flour
1 teaspoon salt
2 cups milk
4 oz. (1 cup) shredded Swiss
   cheese
1 (2-lb.) pkg. frozen hash brown
   potatoes

Heat oven to 350°F. Grease 12x8-inch (2-quart) baking dish. In small bowl, combine Parmesan cheese and parsley; set aside. Melt margarine in large saucepan over medium heat. Stir in flour and salt. Cook until mixture is smooth and bubbly, stirring constantly. Gradually add milk. Cook until mixture boils and slightly thickens, stirring constantly. Remove from heat; stir in Swiss cheese until melted. Add potatoes to Swiss cheese mixture, breaking up clumps of frozen potato if necessary; mix well. Pour into greased baking dish; cover with foil.

Bake at 350°F. for 50 minutes. Remove foil; stir. Sprinkle with Parmesan cheese mixture. Bake uncovered an additional 10 to 15 minutes or until potatoes are tender.

16 (½-cup) servings.

NUTRITION INFORMATION PER SERVING

SERVING SIZE: 1/2 CUP		PERCENT U.S. RDA PER SERVING	
CALORIES	110	PROTEIN	8%
PROTEIN	5g	VITAMIN A	4%
CARBOHYDRATE	13g	VITAMIN C	6%
FAT	5g	THIAMINE	4%
CHOLESTEROL	10mg	RIBOFLAVIN	6%
SODIUM	240mg	NIACIN	4%
POTASSIUM	220mg	CALCIUM	15%
		IRON	4%

There is no potato peeling or mashing for this quick side dish.

ONION 'N' CHIVE MASHED POTATOES

1¼ cups water
2 tablespoons margarine or
   butter
¼ cup finely chopped onion
1 tablespoon chopped fresh
   chives or 1 teaspoon freeze-
   dried chives
¼ teaspoon garlic salt
½ cup milk
½ cup dairy sour cream
1⅓ cups Hungry Jack® Mashed
   Potato Flakes

In medium saucepan, bring water, margarine, onion, chives and garlic salt to a boil. Remove from heat; stir in milk and sour cream. Add potato flakes, stirring with fork until potatoes are desired consistency.

4 (½-cup) servings.

NUTRITION INFORMATION PER SERVING

SERVING SIZE: 1/2 CUP		PERCENT U.S. RDA PER SERVING	
CALORIES	200	PROTEIN	6%
PROTEIN	4g	VITAMIN A	10%
CARBOHYDRATE	18g	VITAMIN C	2%
FAT	13g	THIAMINE	*
CHOLESTEROL	16mg	RIBOFLAVIN	6%
SODIUM	250mg	NIACIN	4%
POTASSIUM	260mg	CALCIUM	8%
		IRON	2%

*Contains less than 2% of the U.S. RDA of this nutrient.

COOK'S NOTE

POTATOES

A favorite comfort food, potatoes are probably the most versatile vegetable in the world and can be cooked in any way imaginable! Familiar potatoes found in the market include:

- Idaho or russet potatoes, which have superior baking and frying qualities.

- All purpose potatoes, which include round potatoes with white or red skins and long potatoes with white skins. These potatoes are excellent for boiling, mashing and salad making.

- New potatoes, which are young red potatoes small enough to cook whole. They are a good choice for potato salads and pan-roasted potatoes.

New varieties may be available in your area. These include baby russet and red potatoes, buttery-tasting yellow Finnish potatoes, snack-sized Texas Finger potatoes and purple potatoes from Peru!

Store potatoes in a cool, dark, well-ventilated place. Refrigerating potatoes causes them to become sweet and to turn dark. Warm temperatures encourage sprouting and shriveling.

RICED POTATOES

This serving variation for potatoes is a tasty alternative to mashed potatoes. Ricing produces potatoes with the texture of soft cooked rice.

To prepare riced potatoes, simply press peeled, freshly cooked hot potatoes through a potato ricer. They are delicious served with gravy and other toppings. Potato ricers are available in housewares departments or at specialty kitchen stores.

Potato Ricer

COUNTRY KITCHEN DESSERTS

These old-fashioned favorites in their new-fashioned versions will win you over.

Who can resist dessert when it's fruity **Gingerbread with Raspberry-Pear Sauce,** creamy **Rice Custard with Pineapple-Apricot Sauce** or melt-in-your-mouth **Chocolate Meringue Dessert?** Our selection of cakes, cobblers, cookies, pies and puddings are reminiscent of days gone by, but we've added twists in preparation and flavor combinations that make them as current as today's fashions. And for a special treat on Valentine's Day, look for the hearts next to recipe names that identify our **Sweetheart Treats.**

This attractive dessert will add a special touch to any dinner party. You will enjoy serving it to your guests.

BAVARIAN APPLE TART

(pictured on p. 62)

CRUST
1½ cups Pillsbury's BEST® All
    Purpose or Unbleached
    Flour
½ cup sugar
½ cup margarine or butter,
    softened
1 egg
¼ teaspoon almond extract

FILLING
½ cup golden or dark raisins
⅓ cup sliced almonds
2 large apples, peeled, cored,
    cut into ¼-inch slices
2 teaspoons cornstarch
¼ cup milk
1 tablespoon lemon juice
¼ teaspoon vanilla
¼ teaspoon almond extract
1 (8-oz.) carton vanilla yogurt
1 egg, beaten
¼ cup apricot preserves, melted

Heat oven to 375°F. Lightly spoon flour into measuring cup; level off. In large bowl, combine flour, sugar and margarine; beat on low speed until well blended. Beat in 1 egg and ¼ teaspoon almond extract to form crumbs. Press crumb mixture in bottom and 1½ inches up sides of ungreased 9-inch springform pan. Sprinkle with raisins and almonds. Arrange apple slices over raisins and almonds in desired pattern.

In medium bowl, dissolve cornstarch in milk. Add lemon juice, vanilla, ¼ teaspoon almond extract, yogurt and 1 beaten egg; blend well. Pour over apples.

Bake at 375°F. for 55 to 65 minutes or until apples are tender. Cool 30 minutes; remove sides of pan. Brush preserves over apples. Garnish with whipped cream, if desired. Refrigerate any remaining tart. 10 to 12 servings.

HIGH ALTITUDE—Above 3500 Feet: No change.

NUTRITION INFORMATION PER SERVING

SERVING SIZE: 1/12 OF RECIPE		PERCENT U.S. RDA PER SERVING	
CALORIES	260	PROTEIN	6%
PROTEIN	5g	VITAMIN A	8%
CARBOHYDRATE	37g	VITAMIN C	2%
FAT	10g	THIAMINE	10%
CHOLESTEROL	37mg	RIBOFLAVIN	10%
SODIUM	115mg	NIACIN	6%
POTASSIUM	180mg	CALCIUM	6%
		IRON	6%

Free yourself from last-minute preparations with this delightful do-ahead dessert.

CHOCOLATE DATE CREAM PIE

CRUST
1¼ cups chocolate wafer cookie
    crumbs (about 22 cookies)
¼ cup sugar
⅓ cup melted margarine or
    butter

FILLING
1 cup dates, cut up
1 cup water
1 cup miniature marshmallows
½ cup chopped walnuts
¼ cup miniature chocolate
    chips
1 cup whipping cream
2 tablespoons powdered sugar
½ teaspoon vanilla
    Sweetened whipped cream, if
    desired
    Walnut halves dipped in
    chocolate, if desired

Heat oven to 375°F. In medium bowl, combine all crust ingredients; blend well. Reserve 2 tablespoons of crumb mixture for garnish. Press remaining mixture in 9-inch pie pan to form crust. Bake at 375°F. for 5 minutes. Cool completely.

In medium saucepan, combine dates and water. Bring to a boil. Reduce heat; simmer 6 to 8 minutes until thickened, stirring occasionally. Remove from heat. Add marshmallows; stir until melted. Cool to room temperature. Stir in chopped walnuts and chocolate chips.

In small bowl, beat 1 cup whipping cream, powdered sugar and vanilla until stiff peaks form. Spread date mixture in cooled crust. Spread whipped cream over top; sprinkle with reserved crumb mixture. Refrigerate until firm, at least 2 hours or overnight. Garnish with dollops of sweetened whipped cream and walnut halves dipped in chocolate. Store in refrigerator. 8 servings.

NUTRITION INFORMATION PER SERVING

SERVING SIZE: 1/8 OF RECIPE		PERCENT U.S. RDA PER SERVING	
CALORIES	450	PROTEIN	6%
PROTEIN	4g	VITAMIN A	15%
CARBOHYDRATE	46g	VITAMIN C	*
FAT	28g	THIAMINE	6%
CHOLESTEROL	47mg	RIBOFLAVIN	6%
SODIUM	125mg	NIACIN	4%
POTASSIUM	250mg	CALCIUM	4%
		IRON	6%

*Contains less than 2% of the U.S. RDA of this nutrient.

This refreshing, crustless pie is a delightful ending to a special dinner.

FROZEN CITRUS CREAM PIE

(pictured on p. 68)

¾ cup sugar
1 cup orange juice
¼ cup lemon juice
1 teaspoon grated orange peel
½ teaspoon grated lemon peel
1 pint (2 cups) whipping cream
¾ cup powdered sugar
¼ teaspoon vanilla
¼ teaspoon almond extract
½ cup maraschino cherries,
    chopped, well drained
½ cup chopped pecans

In small bowl, combine sugar, orange juice and lemon juice; blend well. Let stand 5 minutes or until sugar is dissolved. Add orange peel and lemon peel; blend well. Pour into 9-inch pie pan. Freeze about 1 hour or until firm.

In large bowl, beat whipping cream, powdered sugar, vanilla and almond extract until stiff peaks form. Fold in cherries and pecans. Spread over frozen juice mixture. Freeze until firm, about 4 hours or overnight. Garnish as desired. 8 servings.

NUTRITION INFORMATION PER SERVING

SERVING SIZE: 1/8 OF RECIPE		PERCENT U.S. RDA PER SERVING	
CALORIES	410	PROTEIN	2%
PROTEIN	2g	VITAMIN A	20%
CARBOHYDRATE	39g	VITAMIN C	25%
FAT	27g	THIAMINE	4%
CHOLESTEROL	82mg	RIBOFLAVIN	4%
SODIUM	25mg	NIACIN	*
POTASSIUM	140mg	CALCIUM	4%
		IRON	*

*Contains less than 2% of the U.S. RDA of this nutrient.

❤ SWEETHEART TREATS ❤

Love is a many-splendored thing, so we've created a splendid collection of heart-warming cakes, cookies, pies and dessert garnishes for the loves in your life. Look for these recipes ❤ which showcase the flavors— cherry, chocolate, strawberry, raspberry—and heart shapes, to lusciously say, "I love you."

Old favorites can get better! Juicy red cherries and plump blueberries bake in sweet harmony under a crisp cinnamon sugar pastry. Use your fanciest cutters for pastry designs to add a decorative touch for a special occasion.

CHERRY 'N' BLUEBERRY PIE

❤

1 (15-oz.) pkg. Pillsbury's All Ready Pie Crusts
1 teaspoon flour

FILLING
¾ cup sugar
¼ cup cornstarch
2 (16-oz.) cans pitted, red tart pie cherries, drained, reserving 1 cup liquid
1 tablespoon margarine or butter
1½ cups fresh or frozen blueberries

TOPPING
1 teaspoon milk
1 tablespoon sugar
⅛ teaspoon cinnamon

Prepare pie crust according to package directions for **two-crust pie** using 9-inch pie pan. Heat oven to 400°F.

In medium saucepan, combine sugar and cornstarch. Gradually add reserved 1 cup cherry liquid. Cook over medium heat until mixture just begins to boil, stirring occasionally. Boil 1 minute until thick and clear, stirring constantly. Remove from heat; stir in margarine. Gently stir in cherries. Place blueberries in bottom of pie crust-lined pan. Top with cherry mixture.

Using 1-inch heart-shaped cutter, cut 4 hearts from second crust. Carefully place crust on top of filling; flute. Decorate with heart cutouts. Brush crust and cutouts with milk. In small bowl, combine 1 tablespoon sugar and cinnamon; sprinkle over crust and cutouts. Bake at 400°F. for 40 to 55 minutes or until golden brown.* Cool several hours before serving. 8 servings.

TIP: *Cover edge of pie crust with strip of foil during last 10 to 15 minutes of baking if necessary to prevent excessive browning.

NUTRITION INFORMATION PER SERVING

SERVING SIZE: 1/8 OF RECIPE		PERCENT U.S. RDA PER SERVING	
CALORIES	430	PROTEIN	4%
PROTEIN	3g	VITAMIN A	10%
CARBOHYDRATE	69g	VITAMIN C	6%
FAT	16g	THIAMINE	2%
CHOLESTEROL	14mg	RIBOFLAVIN	4%
SODIUM	230mg	NIACIN	2%
POTASSIUM	190mg	CALCIUM	*
		IRON	6%

*Contains less than 2% of the U.S. RDA of this nutrient.

This spectacular make-ahead dessert is a takeoff on lemon meringue pie. Fluffy meringue is piled high on layers of angel food cake, tangy lemon filling and ice cream.

LEMON MERINGUE BAKED ALASKA

LEMON FILLING
½ **cup sugar**
⅓ **cup lemon juice**
3 **egg yolks**
1 **tablespoon grated lemon peel**

CAKE
1 **loaf angel food cake**
    (approximately 12x5-inches)
½ **gallon brick vanilla ice cream**

MERINGUE
3 **egg whites**
¼ **teaspoon cream of tartar**
1 **teaspoon vanilla**
6 **tablespoons sugar**

In small saucepan, combine all filling ingredients except lemon peel; blend well. Cook over medium-low heat until thickened, about 10 minutes, stirring constantly. Stir in lemon peel. Press plastic wrap onto top of hot filling. Refrigerate until cooled completely.

Slice cake in half horizontally to form 2 layers. Place 1 layer on ungreased cookie sheet. Spread evenly with half of cooled lemon filling. Cut ½-inch slices of ice cream to fit cake layer. Carefully place on top of lemon filling. Repeat layers, ending with ice cream. Cover; freeze 4 hours or overnight until firm. (Freeze remaining ice cream for a later use.)

Heat oven to 450°F. To make meringue, in small bowl beat egg whites, cream of tartar and vanilla at high speed until soft peaks form. Gradually add sugar, 1 tablespoon at a time, beating continuously until stiff peaks form and mixture is glossy. Completely cover frozen loaf with meringue, sealing meringue to cookie sheet.* Bake at 450°F. for 2 to 3 minutes or until lightly browned. Slice and serve immediately. Store in freezer. 12 servings.

▥ MICROWAVE DIRECTIONS: To prepare filling, in 1-quart microwave-safe bowl, combine all filling ingredients except lemon peel; blend well. Microwave on MEDIUM for 4 to 5 minutes or until mixture thickens slightly and starts to boil, whisking twice during cooking. Stir in lemon peel. Press plastic wrap onto top of hot filling. Refrigerate until cooled completely.

TIP: *To make ahead, prepare recipe to * Store in freezer up to 24 hours. Just before serving, heat oven to 450°F. Bake as directed above.

NUTRITION INFORMATION PER SERVING

SERVING SIZE: 1/12 OF RECIPE		PERCENT U.S. RDA PER SERVING	
CALORIES	270	PROTEIN	8%
PROTEIN	6g	VITAMIN A	6%
CARBOHYDRATE	46g	VITAMIN C	2%
FAT	8g	THIAMINE	4%
CHOLESTEROL	81mg	RIBOFLAVIN	15%
SODIUM	150mg	NIACIN	*
POTASSIUM	160mg	CALCIUM	8%
		IRON	2%

*Contains less than 2% of the U.S. RDA of this nutrient.

CHOCOLATE MERINGUE DESSERT

(pictured on left)

MERINGUE
- **6 egg whites**
- **½ teaspoon cream of tartar**
- **¼ teaspoon salt**
- **1½ cups sugar**

FILLING
- **2 (3-oz.) pkg. cream cheese, softened**
- **⅔ cup chocolate-flavored syrup**
- **1 pint (2 cups) whipping cream**
- **1 cup miniature marshmallows**
- **½ cup sliced almonds**
- **⅓ cup chocolate-flavored syrup**

Heat oven to 450°F. Grease 13x9-inch baking pan. In large bowl, beat egg whites, cream of tartar and salt at high speed until soft peaks form. Gradually add sugar, 2 tablespoons at a time, beating continuously until stiff peaks form and mixture is glossy, about 10 minutes. Spread in greased pan. Place in 450°F oven; turn oven off. Leave in closed oven several hours or overnight.

In small bowl, beat cream cheese and ⅔ cup chocolate syrup until smooth. In large bowl, beat whipping cream until stiff peaks form. Fold chocolate mixture and marshmallows into whipped cream. Spread over meringue. Sprinkle with almonds. Refrigerate at least 4 hours. To serve, cut into squares; place on plates. Drizzle each serving with about 1 teaspoon of chocolate syrup. Store in refrigerator. 16 servings.

HIGH ALTITUDE—Above 3500 Feet: No change.

NUTRITION INFORMATION PER SERVING

SERVING SIZE: 1/16 OF RECIPE		PERCENT U.S. RDA PER SERVING	
CALORIES	290	PROTEIN	6%
PROTEIN	4 g	VITAMIN A	10%
CARBOHYDRATE	34 g	VITAMIN C	*
FAT	16 g	THIAMINE	*
CHOLESTEROL	52 mg	RIBOFLAVIN	8%
SODIUM	115 mg	NIACIN	*
POTASSIUM	120 mg	CALCIUM	4%
		IRON	4%

*Contains less than 2% of the U.S. RDA of this nutrient.

Pictured top to bottom: Two-tone Chocolate Filigree Heart, Chocolate Meringue Dessert, Frozen Citrus Cream Pie p. 65

COOK'S NOTE
MAKING CHOCOLATE FILIGREE GARNISHES

Chocolate Filigree Hearts:
To make a pattern, draw a 1 to 1½-inch heart on white paper. Cut twelve 3x3-inch squares of waxed paper.

In small saucepan over low heat, melt ¼ cup semi-sweet chocolate chips or 2 ounces semi-sweet chocolate cut into small pieces with 1½ teaspoons shortening, stirring until melted. Pour melted chocolate into a decorating bag fitted with a small writing tip or into a small heavy-duty plastic bag with small tip cut from one corner. Place a waxed paper square over the heart pattern. Pipe chocolate over the heart design, outlining heart. Carefully slip out pattern piece. Repeat, making 12 hearts. Refrigerate 5 to 10 minutes or until set. Carefully remove from waxed paper or for Two-tone Chocolate Filigree Hearts continue as directed below. Arrange on dessert as desired.

Two-tone Chocolate Filigree Hearts (pictured on left):
To make Two-tone Chocolate Filigree Hearts, prepare the Chocolate Filigree Hearts as directed above.

Melt vanilla-flavored candy coating or flavored chips such as butterscotch or peanut butter. Pour contrasting color/flavor of melted chips into another decorating bag. Pipe desired filigree design inside each Chocolate Filigree Heart. Refrigerate 5 to 10 minutes or until set. Gently remove waxed paper.

Free-Form Chocolate Filigree:
Pipe melted chocolate in zigzag or other free-form design onto waxed paper-lined cookie sheet. Refrigerate until set. Repeat drizzle if desired, piping contrasting color on top of first design to form a two-tone pattern.

All families look forward to dessert. It is like the last act of a play. This happy ending features a pie filled with bananas and a velvety rich chocolate filling swirled with whipped cream.

CHOCOLATE BANANA CREAM PIE

(pictured on right)

1 (15-oz.) pkg. Pillsbury All
  Ready Pie Crusts
1 teaspoon flour

FILLING
1 cup sugar
¼ cup cornstarch
¼ teaspoon salt
3 cups milk
2 oz. (2 squares) unsweetened
  chocolate, cut into pieces
3 egg yolks, slightly beaten
1 tablespoon margarine or
  butter
1 teaspoon vanilla
2 bananas, sliced

TOPPING
1 cup whipping cream
¼ cup powdered sugar

Heat oven to 450°F. Prepare pie crust according to package directions for **unfilled one-crust pie** using 9-inch pie pan. (Refrigerate remaining pie crust for a later use.) Bake at 450°F. for 9 to 11 minutes or until golden brown. Cool completely.

In medium saucepan, combine sugar, cornstarch and salt. Stir in milk and chocolate. Cook over medium heat until mixture boils and thickens, about 15 minutes, stirring frequently. Boil 2 minutes, stirring constantly. Gradually stir ¼ cup of hot mixture into egg yolks; return egg mixture to saucepan. Cook until mixture is bubbly, stirring constantly. Remove from heat; stir in margarine and vanilla. Reserve ¼ cup filling. Press plastic wrap onto top of hot filling in saucepan and reserved ¼ cup filling. Refrigerate 1 hour.

Place bananas in bottom of cooled crust. Pour cooled filling over bananas. In small bowl, beat whipping cream and powdered sugar until stiff peaks form. Spread over filling. Spoon reserved ¼ cup filling by teaspoonfuls over whipped cream. With knife, swirl in circular pattern to marble. Refrigerate 4 hours or until set. Store in refrigerator. 8 to 10 servings.

MICROWAVE DIRECTIONS: To prepare filling in 8-cup microwave-safe measuring cup or large bowl, combine sugar, cornstarch and salt. Stir in milk and chocolate. Microwave on HIGH for 8 to 10 minutes or until mixture comes to a boil, stirring twice during cooking. Stir. Microwave on HIGH for 1 minute. Gradually stir ¼ cup of hot mixture into egg yolks; return egg mixture to measuring cup. Microwave on HIGH for 35 to 55 seconds or until mixture boils. Stir in margarine and vanilla. Microwave on HIGH for 1 minute. Reserve ¼ cup filling. Press plastic wrap onto top of hot filling in measuring cup and reserved ¼ cup filling. Refrigerate 1 hour. Continue as directed above.

NUTRITION INFORMATION PER SERVING

SERVING SIZE: 1/10 OF RECIPE		PERCENT U.S. RDA PER SERVING	
CALORIES	410	PROTEIN	8%
PROTEIN	5g	VITAMIN A	15%
CARBOHYDRATE	47g	VITAMIN C	2%
FAT	22g	THIAMINE	2%
CHOLESTEROL	109mg	RIBOFLAVIN	10%
SODIUM	200mg	NIACIN	*
POTASSIUM	290mg	CALCIUM	10%
		IRON	4%

*Contains less than 2% of the U.S. RDA of this nutrient.

Chocolate Banana Cream Pie

Take this flavorful treat as dessert for a potluck dinner, or bake a pan for the family and freeze a portion of it for later use.

GINGER ORANGE BARS

BARS
½ **cup sugar**
½ **cup margarine or butter, softened**
½ **cup molasses**
1 **egg**
1½ **cups Pillsbury's BEST® All Purpose or Unbleached Flour**
½ **cup Pillsbury's BEST® Whole Wheat Flour**
1 **teaspoon baking soda**
¼ **teaspoon ginger**
⅔ **cup buttermilk***
½ **cup chopped walnuts**
2 **teaspoons grated orange peel**

FROSTING
2 **cups powdered sugar**
2 **tablespoons margarine or butter, softened**
½ **teaspoon grated orange peel**
3 **to 4 tablespoons orange juice**

Heat oven to 350°F. Grease 15x10x1-inch baking pan. In large bowl, combine sugar and ½ cup margarine; beat until light and fluffy. Add molasses and egg; beat well.

Lightly spoon flour into measuring cup; level off. In small bowl, combine all purpose and whole wheat flour, baking soda and ginger; blend well. Add to sugar mixture alternately with buttermilk; mix well. Stir in walnuts and 2 teaspoons orange peel. Spread in greased pan. Bake at 350°F. for 15 to 20 minutes or until toothpick inserted in center comes out clean. Cool.

In small bowl, combine all frosting ingredients, adding enough orange juice for desired spreading consistency. Beat until smooth. Spread over cooled bars. 48 bars.

TIP: *To substitute for buttermilk, use 2 teaspoons vinegar or lemon juice plus milk to make ⅔ cup.

HIGH ALTITUDE—Above 3500 Feet: No change.

NUTRITION INFORMATION PER SERVING

SERVING SIZE: 1 BAR		PERCENT U.S. RDA PER SERVING	
CALORIES	80	PROTEIN	*
PROTEIN	1 g	VITAMIN A	2%
CARBOHYDRATE	13 g	VITAMIN C	*
FAT	3 g	THIAMINE	2%
CHOLESTEROL	5 mg	RIBOFLAVIN	2%
SODIUM	60 mg	NIACIN	*
POTASSIUM	60 mg	CALCIUM	*
		IRON	2%

*Contains less than 2% of the U.S. RDA of this nutrient.

COOK'S NOTE
ALL PURPOSE FLOUR
All purpose flour is milled from the inner part of the wheat kernel and contains neither the germ (the sprouting part) nor the bran (the outer coating). Since 1940, the enrichment of all purpose flour with thiamine, riboflavin, niacin and iron has been encouraged by the U.S. Food and Drug Administration. All purpose flour can be purchased bleached or unbleached. Bleached flour has been whitened by a bleaching agent. They are both suitable for all kinds of baking.

Peanut butter and chocolate are enjoyed by all ages—tiny tots to grown-ups. Serve this great after-school or after-work snack with a glass of cold milk.

PEANUT BUTTER FINGERS

BAR
1 cup Pillsbury's BEST® All Purpose or Unbleached Flour
1 cup rolled oats
½ cup sugar
½ cup firmly packed brown sugar
½ teaspoon baking soda
¼ teaspoon salt
½ cup margarine or butter, softened
⅓ cup peanut butter
½ teaspoon vanilla
1 egg

FROSTING AND GLAZE
1 (6-oz.) pkg. (1 cup) semi-sweet chocolate chips
⅓ cup powdered sugar
2 tablespoons peanut butter
3 to 5 teaspoons milk

Heat oven to 350°F. Grease 13x9-inch pan. Lightly spoon flour into measuring cup; level off. In large bowl, combine all bar ingredients; blend at low speed until mixture forms a soft dough. Press in bottom of greased pan.

Bake at 350°F. for 15 to 20 minutes or until golden brown. Sprinkle immediately with chocolate chips. Let stand 5 minutes; spread evenly to cover. In small bowl, combine remaining glaze ingredients, adding enough milk for desired drizzling consistency; drizzle over chocolate frosting. Cool completely; cut into bars. 36 bars.

HIGH ALTITUDE—Above 3500 Feet: No change.

NUTRITION INFORMATION PER SERVING

SERVING SIZE: 1 BAR		PERCENT U.S. RDA PER SERVING	
CALORIES	120	PROTEIN	2%
PROTEIN	2g	VITAMIN A	2%
CARBOHYDRATE	14g	VITAMIN C	*
FAT	6g	THIAMINE	2%
CHOLESTEROL	6mg	RIBOFLAVIN	2%
SODIUM	80mg	NIACIN	2%
POTASSIUM	65mg	CALCIUM	*
		IRON	2%

*Contains less than 2% of the U.S. RDA of this nutrient.

Crescent rolls are the base for these easy bars.

APRICOT DATE NUT SQUARES

1 (8-oz.) can Pillsbury Refrigerated Quick Crescent Dinner Rolls
¾ cup finely chopped dried apricots
¾ cup finely chopped dates
½ cup chopped walnuts
1 (14-oz.) can sweetened condensed milk (not evaporated)
Powdered sugar

Heat oven to 375°F. Unroll dough into 2 long rectangles. Place in ungreased 13x9-inch pan; press over bottom and ½ inch up sides to form crust. Firmly press perforations to seal. Bake at 375°F. for 5 minutes. Cool 3 minutes.

In large bowl, combine apricots, dates, walnuts and sweetened condensed milk. Spoon mixture evenly over crust. Bake an additional 25 to 30 minutes or until edges are golden brown. Cool completely. Sprinkle with powdered sugar; cut into bars. 36 bars.

NUTRITION INFORMATION PER SERVING

SERVING SIZE: 1 BAR		PERCENT U.S. RDA PER SERVING	
CALORIES	100	PROTEIN	2%
PROTEIN	2g	VITAMIN A	4%
CARBOHYDRATE	16g	VITAMIN C	*
FAT	4g	THIAMINE	2%
CHOLESTEROL	6mg	RIBOFLAVIN	4%
SODIUM	70mg	NIACIN	*
POTASSIUM	140mg	CALCIUM	4%
		IRON	2%

*Contains less than 2% of the U.S. RDA of this nutrient.

This yummy bar, filled with the goodness of raisins and applesauce, is perfect with a hot cup of coffee or tea.

KWIK-KRUMB RAISIN BARS

FILLING
2½ cups raisins
1 cup water
1 cup applesauce
1 teaspoon lemon juice
¼ teaspoon cinnamon

BAR
2 cups rolled oats
1 cup Pillsbury's BEST® All Purpose or Unbleached Flour
½ cup sugar
½ cup coconut
¾ cup margarine or butter

In medium saucepan, bring raisins and water to a boil. Reduce heat; simmer 15 minutes. Drain; stir in applesauce, lemon juice and cinnamon. Set aside.

Heat oven to 350°F. Lightly spoon flour into measuring cup; level off. In large bowl, combine oats, flour, sugar and coconut. Using pastry blender or fork, cut in margarine until mixture resembles coarse crumbs. Reserve 2½ cups of crumb mixture for topping. Press remaining crumb mixture firmly in bottom of ungreased 13x9-inch pan. Spread evenly with filling. Sprinkle with reserved crumb mixture; press lightly.

Bake at 350°F. for 30 to 40 minutes or until light golden brown. Cool completely; cut into bars. 36 bars.

HIGH ALTITUDE—Above 3500 Feet: No change.

NUTRITION INFORMATION PER SERVING

SERVING SIZE: 1 BAR		PERCENT U.S. RDA PER SERVING	
CALORIES	120	PROTEIN	2%
PROTEIN	1g	VITAMIN A	2%
CARBOHYDRATE	18g	VITAMIN C	*
FAT	5g	THIAMINE	4%
CHOLESTEROL	0mg	RIBOFLAVIN	2%
SODIUM	45mg	NIACIN	*
POTASSIUM	105mg	CALCIUM	*
		IRON	2%

*Contains less than 2% of the U.S. RDA of this nutrient.

This gooey brownie is made easy with cake mix.

CHOCOLATE CARAMEL BARS

BASE
1 pkg. Pillsbury Plus® German Chocolate Cake Mix
⅓ cup margarine or butter, softened
1 egg

TOPPING
1 (6-oz.) pkg. (1 cup) semi-sweet chocolate chips
½ cup chopped nuts
¾ cup caramel ice cream topping
3 tablespoons flour

Heat oven to 350°F. Grease and flour 13x9-inch pan. In large bowl, combine cake mix, margarine and egg at low speed until crumbly. Reserve 1 cup crumbs for topping. Press remaining crumb mixture in greased and floured pan.

Bake at 350°F. for 8 to 10 minutes or until base is slightly puffy. Sprinkle with chocolate chips and nuts. In small bowl, combine caramel topping and flour; blend well. Pour over chocolate chips and nuts; sprinkle with reserved crumbs. Bake at 350°F. for 10 to 20 minutes or until chocolate chips are melted and caramel topping begins to bubble. Cool completely; cut into bars. 36 bars.

HIGH ALTITUDE—Above 3500 Feet: No change.

NUTRITION INFORMATION PER SERVING

SERVING SIZE: 1 BAR		PERCENT U.S. RDA PER SERVING	
CALORIES	130	PROTEIN	2%
PROTEIN	2g	VITAMIN A	*
CARBOHYDRATE	19g	VITAMIN C	*
FAT	6g	THIAMINE	2%
CHOLESTEROL	6mg	RIBOFLAVIN	2%
SODIUM	120mg	NIACIN	*
POTASSIUM	45mg	CALCIUM	*
		IRON	2%

*Contains less than 2% of the U.S. RDA of this nutrient.

This is a great lunch box cookie.

CHEWY GRANOLA COOKIES

1½ cups Pillsbury's BEST® All
    Purpose or Unbleached
    Flour
3 cups rolled oats
1 cup wheat germ
1 teaspoon baking powder
½ teaspoon salt
1 cup firmly packed brown
    sugar
1 cup margarine or butter,
    softened
½ cup honey
1½ teaspoons vanilla
2 eggs
½ cup raisins
½ cup chopped almonds
¼ cup sesame seeds
¼ cup shelled sunflower seeds

Heat oven to 375°F. Lightly grease cookie sheets. Lightly spoon flour into measuring cup; level off. In medium bowl, combine flour, oats, wheat germ, baking powder and salt; mix well. Set aside. In large bowl, beat brown sugar, margarine and honey until light and fluffy. Add vanilla and eggs; blend well. Add flour mixture; mix well. Stir in raisins, almonds, sesame seeds and sunflower seeds. Drop by rounded teaspoonfuls onto greased cookie sheets. Bake at 375°F. for 7 to 8 minutes or until edges are light golden brown. Immediately remove from cookie sheets. 5 dozen cookies.

HIGH ALTITUDE—Above 3500 Feet: No change.

NUTRITION INFORMATION PER SERVING

SERVING SIZE: 1 COOKIE		PERCENT U.S. RDA PER SERVING	
CALORIES	100	PROTEIN	2%
PROTEIN	2g	VITAMIN A	2%
CARBOHYDRATE	13g	VITAMIN C	*
FAT	5g	THIAMINE	6%
CHOLESTEROL	7mg	RIBOFLAVIN	2%
SODIUM	65mg	NIACIN	2%
POTASSIUM	75mg	CALCIUM	*
		IRON	4%

*Contains less than 2% of the U.S. RDA of this nutrient.

Traditional yet trendy! This variation of the ever-popular chocolate chip cookie will satisfy both down-home and sophisticated tastes.

WHITE CHOCOLATE MACADAMIA NUT COOKIES

¾ cup firmly packed brown
    sugar
½ cup sugar
½ cup margarine or butter,
    softened
½ cup shortening
2 teaspoons vanilla
1 egg
1¾ cups Pillsbury's BEST® All
    Purpose or Unbleached
    Flour
1 teaspoon baking soda
½ teaspoon salt
8 oz. vanilla-flavored candy
    coating, coarsely chopped,
    or 1⅓ cups vanilla milk
    chips
1 (3½-oz.) jar macadamia nuts,
    coarsely chopped

Heat oven to 375°F. In large bowl, beat brown sugar, sugar, margarine and shortening until light and fluffy. Add vanilla and egg; blend well. Lightly spoon flour into measuring cup; level off. Stir in flour, baking soda and salt; mix well. Stir in candy coating and macadamia nuts. Drop dough by tablespoonfuls 3 inches apart onto ungreased cookie sheets.

Bake at 375°F. for 8 to 10 minutes or until light golden brown. Cool 1 minute; remove from cookie sheets. 4 dozen cookies.

HIGH ALTITUDE—Above 3500 Feet: Decrease margarine to 6 tablespoons. Decrease baking soda to ¾ teaspoon. Bake as directed above.

NUTRITION INFORMATION PER SERVING

SERVING SIZE: 1 COOKIE		PERCENT U.S. RDA PER SERVING	
CALORIES	120	PROTEIN	*
PROTEIN	1g	VITAMIN A	*
CARBOHYDRATE	12g	VITAMIN C	*
FAT	8g	THIAMINE	2%
CHOLESTEROL	4mg	RIBOFLAVIN	2%
SODIUM	75mg	NIACIN	*
POTASSIUM	35mg	CALCIUM	*
		IRON	2%

*Contains less than 2% of the U.S. RDA of this nutrient.

Give a basket of these colorful, tasty hearts for a very special homemade treat.

VALENTINE ROLLED COOKIES

(pictured on p. 77)

♥

1 cup sugar
1 cup margarine or butter, softened
3 tablespoons milk
1 teaspoon vanilla
1 egg
3 cups Pillsbury's BEST® All Purpose or Unbleached Flour
1½ teaspoons baking powder
½ teaspoon salt
½ teaspoon peppermint extract
¼ to ½ teaspoon red food color
Sugar, if desired

In large bowl, combine 1 cup sugar, margarine, milk, vanilla and egg; blend well. Lightly spoon flour into measuring cup; level off. Add flour, baking powder and salt; mix well.

Divide dough in half; refrigerate one half. To other half of dough, add ½ teaspoon peppermint extract and red food color for desired color. Refrigerate at least 1 hour for easier handling.

Heat oven to 400°F. On lightly floured surface, roll ⅓ of white dough to ⅛-inch thickness. Cut with floured 2½-inch heart-shaped cookie cutter. Place 1 inch apart on ungreased cookie sheets. Repeat with ⅓ of pink dough. Using floured 1-inch heart-shaped cookie cutter, cut center from each pink and white cookie. Remove centers. Replace each center in cookie of opposite colored dough. Sprinkle with sugar. Repeat with remaining dough.

Bake at 400°F. for 5 to 9 minutes or until edges are light golden brown. Cool 1 minute; remove from cookie sheets. Cool on wire rack.
5 to 6 dozen cookies.

HIGH ALTITUDE—Above 3500 Feet: Increase flour to 3 cups plus 2 tablespoons. Bake as directed above.

NUTRITION INFORMATION PER SERVING

SERVING SIZE: 1 COOKIE		PERCENT U.S. RDA PER SERVING	
CALORIES	60	PROTEIN	*
PROTEIN	1 g	VITAMIN A	2%
CARBOHYDRATE	7 g	VITAMIN C	*
FAT	3 g	THIAMINE	2%
CHOLESTEROL	3 mg	RIBOFLAVIN	*
SODIUM	50 mg	NIACIN	*
POTASSIUM	10 mg	CALCIUM	*
		IRON	*

*Contains less than 2% of the U.S. RDA of this nutrient.

Pictured on previous page, top to bottom: Chocolate Cherry Surprise Cookies, Valentine Rolled Cookies

For chocolate and cherry lovers, this is a delicious adaptation of the famous German Black Forest cake. You won't stop at just one cookie!

CHOCOLATE CHERRY SURPRISE COOKIES

(pictured on p. 77)

♥

COOKIES
¾ cup sugar
¼ cup firmly packed brown
  sugar
½ cup margarine or butter,
  softened
½ teaspoon almond extract
1 egg
1¾ cups Pillsbury's BEST® All
  Purpose or Unbleached
  Flour
½ cup unsweetened cocoa
½ teaspoon baking soda
¼ teaspoon salt
½ cup milk
½ cup chopped walnuts
18 to 20 maraschino cherries,
  halved, drained
18 to 20 large marshmallows,
  halved

FROSTING
3 cups powdered sugar
3 tablespoons margarine or
  butter, melted
½ teaspoon vanilla
3 oz. (3 squares) semi-sweet
  chocolate, melted
5 to 6 tablespoons water

Heat oven to 375°F. In large bowl, combine sugar, brown sugar, ½ cup margarine, almond extract and egg; blend well. Lightly spoon flour into measuring cup; level off. In small bowl, combine flour, cocoa, baking soda and salt; blend well. Add to sugar mixture alternately with milk, mixing well after each addition. Stir in walnuts. Drop by rounded tablespoonfuls 2 inches apart onto ungreased cookie sheets. Firmly press cherry half, cut side down, into top of each cookie.

Bake at 375°F. for 6 to 8 minutes. Firmly press marshmallow half, cut side down, over cherry on top of each hot cookie. Bake an additional 2 minutes or until marshmallows are puffed. Let cool 1 minute; remove from cookie sheets. Cool completely.

In small bowl, combine all frosting ingredients, adding enough water for desired spreading consistency. Blend until smooth. Frost top of each cookie with about 2 teaspoonfuls frosting, covering marshmallow completely.* 3 dozen cookies.

TIP: *If frosting becomes too thick to spread easily, stir in a few more drops of water.

HIGH ALTITUDE—Above 3500 Feet: Increase flour to 2 cups. Bake as directed above.

NUTRITION INFORMATION PER SERVING

SERVING SIZE: 1 COOKIE		PERCENT U.S. RDA PER SERVING	
CALORIES	150	PROTEIN	2%
PROTEIN	2g	VITAMIN A	2%
CARBOHYDRATE	25g	VITAMIN C	*
FAT	6g	THIAMINE	4%
CHOLESTEROL	6mg	RIBOFLAVIN	2%
SODIUM	85mg	NIACIN	2%
POTASSIUM	45mg	CALCIUM	*
		IRON	2%

*Contains less than 2% of the U.S. RDA of this nutrient.

APPLE STREUSEL BREAD PUDDING

PUDDING
- 4 cups French bread cubes (1-inch)
- 1 cup chunky applesauce
- ¼ cup raisins
- ¼ teaspoon cinnamon
- ⅛ teaspoon nutmeg
- 2 eggs
- 2 cups milk
- ⅓ cup sugar
- ½ teaspoon cinnamon
- ½ teaspoon vanilla

STREUSEL TOPPING
- ¼ cup flour
- ¼ cup firmly packed brown sugar
- 2 tablespoons margarine or butter

Heat oven to 350°F. Grease 8-inch (square) baking dish or 2-quart casserole. Place 3 cups of the bread cubes in greased dish. In small bowl, combine applesauce, raisins, ¼ teaspoon cinnamon and nutmeg; blend well. Spoon by scant teaspoonfuls over bread cubes. Top with remaining 1 cup bread cubes. Beat eggs in medium bowl. Add milk, sugar, ½ teaspoon cinnamon and vanilla; blend well. Pour over bread cubes; let stand 10 minutes.

In small bowl, combine flour and brown sugar; mix well. With fork or pastry blender, cut in margarine until mixture is crumbly. Sprinkle over top of bread cube mixture. Bake at 350°F. for 50 to 60 minutes or until knife inserted in center comes out clean. Let stand 10 minutes before serving. Serve warm with cream, if desired. Refrigerate any remaining pudding. 8 servings.

NUTRITION INFORMATION PER SERVING

SERVING SIZE: 1/8 OF RECIPE		PERCENT U.S. RDA PER SERVING	
CALORIES	270	PROTEIN	10%
PROTEIN	7g	VITAMIN A	10%
CARBOHYDRATE	42g	VITAMIN C	*
FAT	9g	THIAMINE	10%
CHOLESTEROL	165mg	RIBOFLAVIN	15%
SODIUM	190mg	NIACIN	4%
POTASSIUM	210mg	CALCIUM	10%
		IRON	10%

*Contains less than 2% of the U.S. RDA of this nutrient.

Who doesn't fondly remember apple crisp served warm from the oven with a generous scoop of ice cream? The addition of pear and banana slices makes this crisp even more scrumptious!

FRUIT CRISP

- 4 cups (4 medium) sliced peeled apples
- 2 cups (2 medium) sliced peeled pears
- 1 firm banana, sliced
- 2 tablespoons lemon juice
- 1 cup Pillsbury's BEST® All Purpose or Unbleached Flour
- 1 cup sugar
- 1 teaspoon baking powder
- ½ teaspoon salt
- 1 egg, beaten
- ½ cup margarine or butter, melted
- Cinnamon

Heat oven to 375°F. In large bowl, toss apples, pears and banana with lemon juice. Place in ungreased 12x8-inch baking dish or 9-inch square baking pan.

Lightly spoon flour into measuring cup; level off. In medium bowl, combine flour, sugar, baking powder and salt; mix well. Using fork, toss beaten egg with flour mixture (mixture will be dry). Sprinkle evenly over fruit. Drizzle margarine over flour mixture; sprinkle with cinnamon.

Bake at 375°F. for 35 to 40 minutes or until golden brown and fruit is tender. Serve warm with vanilla ice cream or cream. 10 to 12 servings.

HIGH ALTITUDE—Above 3500 Feet: No change.

NUTRITION INFORMATION PER SERVING

SERVING SIZE: 1/12 OF RECIPE		PERCENT U.S. RDA PER SERVING	
CALORIES	220	PROTEIN	2%
PROTEIN	2g	VITAMIN A	6%
CARBOHYDRATE	37g	VITAMIN C	4%
FAT	8g	THIAMINE	6%
CHOLESTEROL	18mg	RIBOFLAVIN	6%
SODIUM	210mg	NIACIN	2%
POTASSIUM	140mg	CALCIUM	2%
		IRON	4%

To simplify the preparation of traditional rice pudding, we've used cooked rice. For a refreshing flavor change, we've served the pudding with a warm fruit sauce.

RICE CUSTARD WITH PINEAPPLE-APRICOT SAUCE

3 cups warm cooked rice
½ cup sugar
½ teaspoon salt
3 cups milk
2 eggs, slightly beaten
½ teaspoon vanilla
½ teaspoon almond extract

PINEAPPLE-APRICOT SAUCE
1 (8-oz.) can apricots, drained, reserving liquid
⅓ cup firmly packed brown sugar
1 tablespoon cornstarch
2 tablespoons lemon juice
1 (8-oz.) can crushed pineapple, undrained

In large saucepan, combine rice, sugar, salt, milk and eggs. Cook over medium-low heat until slightly thickened, about 20 to 25 minutes, stirring frequently. DO NOT BOIL. Stir in vanilla and almond extract.

To prepare sauce, chop apricots; place in small saucepan. Add reserved apricot liquid and remaining sauce ingredients; blend well. Cook over medium heat until mixture boils, about 7 minutes, stirring frequently. Reduce heat; simmer 2 to 3 minutes or until thickened, stirring occasionally. Serve over custard. Serve custard and sauce warm or cold. Store in refrigerator. 10 (½-cup) servings.

▤ MICROWAVE DIRECTIONS: To prepare sauce, chop apricots; place in 4-cup microwave-safe measuring cup. Add reserved apricot liquid and remaining sauce ingredients; blend well. Microwave on HIGH for 5 to 6 minutes or until mixture thickens and boils, stirring once halfway through cooking.

NUTRITION INFORMATION PER SERVING

SERVING SIZE: 1/10 OF RECIPE		PERCENT U.S. RDA PER SERVING	
CALORIES	220	PROTEIN	8%
PROTEIN	6g	VITAMIN A	10%
CARBOHYDRATE	45g	VITAMIN C	4%
FAT	3g	THIAMINE	10%
CHOLESTEROL	48mg	RIBOFLAVIN	10%
SODIUM	160mg	NIACIN	6%
POTASSIUM	240mg	CALCIUM	10%
		IRON	6%

The combination of two fruit flavors makes this a refreshing finale to a meal. For an extra touch, top each serving with a scoop of vanilla ice cream and a dollop of whipped cream or vanilla yogurt.

CHERRY ORANGE CRISP

1 cup Pillsbury's BEST® All Purpose or Unbleached Flour
½ cup rolled oats
½ cup firmly packed brown sugar
½ cup margarine or butter
1 (21-oz.) can cherry fruit pie filling
½ cup orange marmalade
½ cup sliced almonds

Heat oven to 375°F. Grease 8-inch (2-quart) square baking dish. Lightly spoon flour into measuring cup; level off. In medium bowl, combine flour, rolled oats and brown sugar; blend well. Using fork or pastry blender, cut in margarine until mixture is crumbly. Place pie filling in greased dish. Top with orange marmalade and almonds. Sprinkle flour mixture evenly over fruit.

Bake at 375°F. for 20 to 30 minutes or until golden brown. Serve warm.

HIGH ALTITUDE—Above 3500 Feet: No change.

NUTRITION INFORMATION PER SERVING

SERVING SIZE: 1/9 OF RECIPE		PERCENT U.S. RDA PER SERVING	
CALORIES	430	PROTEIN	6%
PROTEIN	5g	VITAMIN A	10%
CARBOHYDRATE	70g	VITAMIN C	4%
FAT	16g	THIAMINE	10%
CHOLESTEROL	0mg	RIBOFLAVIN	10%
SODIUM	130mg	NIACIN	6%
POTASSIUM	210mg	CALCIUM	6%
		IRON	10%

This heart-shaped Valentine's Day dessert features a buttery crust and cream puff shell piled "mile high" with whipped cream and fresh ripe strawberries—all in a heart shape!

STRAWBERRY CREAM PUFF

(pictured on right)

CRUST
- ⅔ cup Pillsbury's BEST® All Purpose or Unbleached Flour
- ⅓ cup margarine or butter
- 2 to 5 teaspoons ice water

PUFF
- ½ cup water
- ¼ cup margarine or butter
- ½ cup Pillsbury's BEST® All Purpose or Unbleached Flour
- 2 eggs

FILLING
- 1 cup whipping cream
- ⅓ cup powdered sugar
- ¼ cup dairy sour cream
- 1 pint (2 cups) sliced fresh strawberries*

GLAZE
- 2 tablespoons semi-sweet chocolate chips
- 1 tablespoon margarine or butter

Cut heart-shaped pattern about 10 inches long and 9 inches wide from waxed paper or aluminum foil. Heat oven to 375°F. Lightly spoon flour into measuring cup; level off. Place ⅔ cup flour in small bowl. Using fork or pastry blender, cut ⅓ cup margarine into flour until mixture resembles fine crumbs. Sprinkle with ice water, 1 teaspoon at a time, tossing lightly with fork until mixture is moistened and soft dough forms.

Place dough on ungreased cookie sheet. Place pattern over dough. Using pattern as a guide, press dough evenly into heart shape; remove pattern.

In medium saucepan, combine ½ cup water and ¼ cup margarine. Bring to a boil over medium heat. Stir in ½ cup flour. Cook until mixture leaves sides of pan in smooth ball, stirring constantly. Remove from heat. Add eggs 1 at a time, beating vigorously after each addition until mixture is smooth and glossy. With back of spoon, spread puff mixture over crust to within ¾ inch of edge of crust, building up sides and shaping into heart.

Strawberry Cream Puff

Bake at 375°F. for 20 minutes. Remove from oven. With fork, prick center of puff once. Bake an additional 20 to 30 minutes or until deep golden brown and puffed. Cool completely on cookie sheet.

To assemble, slide cooled puff shell onto serving plate. In small bowl, beat whipping cream and sugar until stiff peaks form. Fold in sour cream. Spoon into puff shell. Arrange strawberries in heart shape, overlapping slightly, over whipped cream mixture. In small saucepan over low heat, melt chocolate chips and 1 tablespoon margarine; stir until smooth. Drizzle over strawberries. Serve immediately. Store in refrigerator. 8 to 10 servings.

TIP: *Sliced peaches, grapes, nectarines or raspberries can be substituted.

HIGH ALTITUDE—Above 3500 Feet: No change.

NUTRITION INFORMATION PER SERVING

SERVING SIZE: 1/10 OF RECIPE		PERCENT U.S. RDA PER SERVING	
CALORIES	300	PROTEIN	6%
PROTEIN	4g	VITAMIN A	20%
CARBOHYDRATE	19g	VITAMIN C	30%
FAT	24g	THIAMINE	8%
CHOLESTEROL	78mg	RIBOFLAVIN	10%
SODIUM	160mg	NIACIN	4%
POTASSIUM	120mg	CALCIUM	4%
		IRON	6%

Cake is often the dessert served for celebrations or special occasions. Make this old-fashioned chocolate buttermilk cake with cherry frosting for a Valentine's Day party.

DELICIOUS DEVIL'S FOOD CAKE

CAKE
1½ cups Pillsbury BEST® All
    Purpose or Unbleached
    Flour
1¼ cups sugar
½ cup unsweetened cocoa
1¼ teaspoons baking soda
1 teaspoon salt
1 cup buttermilk*
⅔ cup oil
1 teaspoon vanilla
2 eggs

CHERRY FROSTING
⅔ cup butter or margarine,
    softened
4 cups powdered sugar
2 to 4 tablespoons half-and-half
    or milk
1 teaspoon vanilla
3 tablespoons drained chopped
    maraschino cherries

Heat oven to 350°F. Grease and lightly flour bottoms only of two 8-inch round cake pans. Lightly spoon flour into measuring cup; level off. In large bowl, blend all cake ingredients at low speed until moistened; beat 3 minutes at medium speed. Pour into greased and floured pans. Bake at 350°F. for 25 to 30 minutes or until toothpick inserted in center comes out clean. Cool 5 minutes; remove from pans. Cool completely.

In large bowl, beat butter until light and fluffy. Gradually add powdered sugar, beating well after each addition. Add half-and-half 1 tablespoon at a time, beating well after each addition, until frosting is desired spreading consistency. Stir in cherries. Fill and frost cake. Garnish as desired. 12 servings.

TIP: *To substitute for buttermilk, use 1 tablespoon vinegar or lemon juice plus milk to make 1 cup.

HIGH ALTITUDE—Above 3500 Feet: Increase flour to 1½ cups plus 3 tablespoons. Bake at 375°F. for 25 to 30 minutes.

NUTRITION INFORMATION PER SERVING

SERVING SIZE: 1/12 OF RECIPE		PERCENT U.S. RDA PER SERVING	
CALORIES	520	PROTEIN	6%
PROTEIN	4g	VITAMIN A	8%
CARBOHYDRATE	70g	VITAMIN C	*
FAT	25g	THIAMINE	8%
CHOLESTEROL	66mg	RIBOFLAVIN	10%
SODIUM	460mg	NIACIN	4%
POTASSIUM	95mg	CALCIUM	4%
		IRON	6%

*Contains less than 2% of the U.S. RDA of this nutrient.

PEACH 'N' BLUEBERRY BISCUIT COBBLER

¼ cup water
3 tablespoons cornstarch
5 cups (5 medium) peeled,
    sliced fresh or frozen
    peaches
2 cups fresh or frozen
    blueberries
1¼ cups sugar
¼ teaspoon salt
¼ teaspoon cinnamon
½ cup slivered almonds

TOPPING
1 (10-oz.) can Hungry Jack®
    Refrigerated Flaky Biscuits
½ cup sugar
1 teaspoon cinnamon
2 tablespoons margarine or
    butter, melted
¼ cup slivered almonds

Heat oven to 350°F. In large saucepan, combine water and cornstarch; add peaches, blueberries, 1¼ cups sugar, salt, ¼ teaspoon cinnamon and ½ cup almonds. Cook over medium heat 15 minutes or until mixture is thick and bubbly, stirring constantly. Pour into ungreased 13x9-inch pan.

Separate dough into biscuits. In small bowl, combine ½ cup sugar and 1 teaspoon cinnamon for topping. Dip each biscuit in margarine, then in sugar mixture. Arrange biscuits over hot fruit mixture. Sprinkle with ¼ cup almonds and any remaining sugar mixture. Bake at 350°F. for 20 to 28 minutes or until biscuits are deep golden brown. 10 servings.

TIP: If desired, cobbler can be glazed. In small bowl, combine ½ cup powdered sugar and 2 to 3 teaspoons milk, adding enough milk for desired drizzling consistency. Drizzle over warm biscuits.

NUTRITION INFORMATION PER SERVING

SERVING SIZE: 1/10 OF RECIPE		PERCENT U.S. RDA PER SERVING	
CALORIES	370	PROTEIN	6%
PROTEIN	4g	VITAMIN A	10%
CARBOHYDRATE	65g	VITAMIN C	10%
FAT	11g	THIAMINE	8%
CHOLESTEROL	0mg	RIBOFLAVIN	10%
SODIUM	380mg	NIACIN	10%
POTASSIUM	290mg	CALCIUM	4%
		IRON	8%

Although shortcakes are usually as seasonal as the fruits that dress them, this dessert, made with peach gelatin and yogurt, can be served at any time of the year.

PEACHES AND CREAM SHORTCAKE

1 pkg. Pillsbury Plus® Yellow
    Cake Mix
1 (3-oz.) pkg. peach flavored
    gelatin
⅓ cup water
1 (8-oz.) carton vanilla or peach
    yogurt
3 eggs
1 cup water
1 (4-oz.) carton frozen whipped
    topping, thawed
    Peach slices

Heat oven to 350°F. Grease 13x9-inch pan. In large bowl, combine cake mix, **2 tablespoons** of the gelatin, ⅓ cup water, yogurt and eggs at low speed until moistened. Beat 2 minutes at high speed. Pour into greased pan.

Bake at 350°F. for 30 to 40 minutes or until toothpick inserted in center comes out clean. Cool cake in pan on cooling rack 15 minutes. Meanwhile, in small saucepan heat 1 cup water. Add remaining gelatin; stir to dissolve. Using long-tined fork, prick cake at ½-inch intervals. Pour gelatin mixture evenly over cake; refrigerate. Serve with whipped topping and peach slices. 12 servings.

HIGH ALTITUDE—Above 3500 Feet: Add 2 tablespoons flour to dry cake mix. Increase water in cake to ½ cup. Bake at 375°F. for 25 to 30 minutes.

NUTRITION INFORMATION PER SERVING

SERVING SIZE: 1/12 OF RECIPE		PERCENT U.S. RDA PER SERVING	
CALORIES	280	PROTEIN	8%
PROTEIN	5g	VITAMIN A	6%
CARBOHYDRATE	47g	VITAMIN C	*
FAT	9g	THIAMINE	8%
CHOLESTEROL	54mg	RIBOFLAVIN	10%
SODIUM	320mg	NIACIN	4%
POTASSIUM	130mg	CALCIUM	10%
		IRON	4%

*Contains less than 2% of the U.S. RDA of this nutrient.

Gingerbread—classic, yet classy! Experience the unique flavor combination of red raspberries and pears served over wedges of traditional gingerbread.

GINGERBREAD WITH RASPBERRY-PEAR SAUCE

(pictured on left)

GINGERBREAD
1⅓ cups Pillsbury's BEST® All Purpose or Unbleached Flour
½ cup firmly packed brown sugar
½ teaspoon baking powder
½ teaspoon baking soda
¼ teaspoon salt
¾ teaspoon cinnamon
½ teaspoon ginger
½ cup shortening or margarine
½ cup boiling water
½ cup molasses
1 egg, slightly beaten

RASPBERRY-PEAR SAUCE
1 (10-oz.) pkg. frozen raspberries, thawed
¼ cup sugar
1 tablespoon lemon juice
3 firm pears, peeled, cored, cut into ½-inch pieces (about 3 cups)

Heat oven to 350°F. Grease bottom only of 9-inch round pan. Lightly spoon flour into measuring cup; level off. In large bowl, combine flour, brown sugar, baking powder, baking soda, salt, cinnamon and ginger; mix well. Add remaining gingerbread ingredients; blend well. Pour batter into greased pan. Bake at 350°F. for 25 to 35 minutes or until toothpick inserted in center comes out clean.

Drain raspberries, reserving ¼ cup liquid. In blender container or food processor bowl with metal blade, blend raspberries and reserved ¼ cup liquid at highest speed until smooth. Press through large strainer to remove seeds; discard seeds. In large skillet, combine raspberry puree, sugar, lemon juice and pears. Bring to a boil. Reduce heat; simmer until pears are tender. Serve sauce warm or cool over wedges of gingerbread. Garnish each serving with sweetened whipped cream, if desired. 8 servings.

MICROWAVE DIRECTIONS: To prepare gingerbread, prepare batter as directed above. Pour into ungreased 8-inch round microwave-safe dish. Microwave on HIGH for 5 to 7 minutes or until toothpick inserted in center comes out clean. Cool directly on counter for 10 minutes.

To prepare sauce, prepare raspberry puree as directed above; combine with sugar, lemon juice and pears in medium microwave-safe bowl or 8-cup microwave-safe measuring cup. Microwave on HIGH for 5 to 6 minutes or until pears are tender, stirring twice during cooking. Serve as directed above.

HIGH ALTITUDE—Above 3500 Feet. Increase flour to 1⅔ cups. Decrease brown sugar to ¼ cup. Bake or microwave as directed above.

NUTRITION INFORMATION PER SERVING

SERVING SIZE: 1/8 OF RECIPE		PERCENT U.S. RDA PER SERVING	
CALORIES	410	PROTEIN	4%
PROTEIN	3g	VITAMIN A	*
CARBOHYDRATE	67g	VITAMIN C	10%
FAT	14g	THIAMINE	15%
CHOLESTEROL	27mg	RIBOFLAVIN	10%
SODIUM	170mg	NIACIN	8%
POTASSIUM	420mg	CALCIUM	10%
		IRON	20%

*Contains less than 2% of the U.S. RDA of this nutrient.

Gingerbread with Raspberry-Pear Sauce

A piña colada is a delicious drink made with coconut, pineapple juice and rum. These tropical ingredients make this moist poke-and-pour cake delicious and extra special.

PIÑA COLADA PARTY CAKE

1 cup coconut
1 pkg. Pillsbury Plus® White
  Cake Mix
½ cup water
½ cup pineapple juice
⅓ cup oil
¼ cup rum*
4 egg whites
½ cup pineapple juice
½ cup sugar

FROSTING
1 can Pillsbury Vanilla Frosting
  Supreme™
1 tablespoon rum or ½ teaspoon
  rum extract
½ cup reserved toasted coconut

Heat oven to 350°F. On cookie sheet, toast 1 cup coconut at 350°F. for 5 to 7 minutes. Reserve ½ cup for frosting. Grease and flour 13x9-inch pan. In large bowl, blend cake mix, water, ½ cup pineapple juice, oil, ¼ cup rum and egg whites at low speed until moistened; beat 2 minutes at high speed. Stir in ½ cup coconut. Pour into greased and floured pan.

Bake at 350°F. for 25 to 35 minutes or until toothpick inserted in center comes out clean. Cool 10 minutes. In small saucepan, heat ½ cup pineapple juice and sugar to boiling. Using long-tined fork, prick cake at ½-inch intervals. Pour hot pineapple mixture over cake. Cool completely.

In small bowl, blend frosting and 1 tablespoon rum. Frost cake; sprinkle with ½ cup reserved coconut. Refrigerate until serving. 12 servings.

TIP: *To substitute for rum, use ¼ cup water and 1 teaspoon rum extract.

HIGH ALTITUDE—Above 3500 Feet: Add 3 tablespoons flour to dry cake mix. Increase water to ½ cup plus 1 tablespoon. Bake at 375°F. for 25 to 35 minutes.

NUTRITION INFORMATION PER SERVING

SERVING SIZE: 1/12 OF RECIPE		PERCENT U.S. RDA PER SERVING	
CALORIES	490	PROTEIN	4%
PROTEIN	3g	VITAMIN A	*
CARBOHYDRATE	73g	VITAMIN C	2%
FAT	20g	THIAMINE	6%
CHOLESTEROL	0mg	RIBOFLAVIN	8%
SODIUM	360mg	NIACIN	4%
POTASSIUM	110mg	CALCIUM	8%
		IRON	4%

*Contains less than 2% of the U.S. RDA of this nutrient.

Ah, apple cake! This dessert is chock full of apples and can be served with a variety of toppings—a sprinkling of powdered sugar, a dollop of whipped cream or a scoop of ice cream drizzled with caramel sauce.

LOTS O' APPLE CAKE

1⅓ cups Pillsbury's BEST® All Purpose or Unbleached Flour
1 cup Pillsbury's BEST® Whole Wheat Flour
1¼ cups sugar
2 teaspoons baking soda
1 teaspoon salt
1 teaspoon cinnamon
5 cups (5 medium) thinly sliced peeled apples
½ cup oil
¼ cup honey
1 teaspoon vanilla
2 eggs or ½ cup frozen cholesterol-free egg product, thawed
½ cup chopped nuts

Heat oven to 350°F. Grease and flour bottom only of 13x9-inch pan. Lightly spoon flour into measuring cup; level off. In large bowl, combine all ingredients except nuts; blend at low speed until moistened. Beat 2 minutes at medium speed. Stir in nuts. Spread in greased and floured pan.

Bake at 350°F. for 40 to 50 minutes or until toothpick inserted in center comes out clean. Serve warm or cool. Store cake in refrigerator. 12 servings.

HIGH ALTITUDE—Above 3500 Feet: Increase all purpose flour to 1⅓ cups plus 2 tablespoons. Bake as directed above.

NUTRITION INFORMATION PER SERVING

SERVING SIZE: 1/12 OF RECIPE		PERCENT U.S. RDA PER SERVING	
CALORIES	340	PROTEIN	6%
PROTEIN	5g	VITAMIN A	*
CARBOHYDRATE	52g	VITAMIN C	2%
FAT	13g	THIAMINE	10%
CHOLESTEROL	35mg	RIBOFLAVIN	8%
SODIUM	380mg	NIACIN	8%
POTASSIUM	150mg	CALCIUM	*
		IRON	8%

*Contains less than 2% of the U.S. RDA of this nutrient.

NUTRITION INFORMATION

Nutrition Information: Pillsbury recipe analysis is provided per serving or per unit of food and is based on the most current nutritional values available from the United States Department of Agriculture (USDA) and food manufacturers. Each recipe is calculated for number of calories; grams of protein, carbohydrate and fat; and milligrams of cholesterol, sodium and potassium.

Vitamin and mineral levels are stated as percentages of United States Recommended Daily Allowances. RDAs are the dietary standards determined by the U.S. Food and Drug Administration for healthy people. If you are following a medically prescribed diet, consult your physician or registered dietitian about using this nutrition information.

Calculating Nutrition Information: Recipe analysis is calculated on:

• A single serving based on the largest number of servings, or on a specific amount (1 tablespoon) or unit (1 cookie).

• The first ingredient or amount when more than one is listed.

• "If desired" or garnishing ingredients when they are included in the ingredient listing.

• Only the amount of a marinade or frying oil absorbed during preparation.

Using Nutrition Information: The amount of nutrients a person needs is determined by one's age, size and activity level. The following are general guidelines you can use for evaluating your daily food intake:

Calories: 2350
Protein: 45 to 65 grams
Carbohydrates: 340 grams
Fat: 80 grams or less
Cholesterol: 300 milligrams or less
Sodium: 2400 milligrams

A nutritionally balanced diet recommends limiting intake of fat to 30 percent or less of total daily calories. One gram of fat is 9 calories. You can determine the fat content of recipes or products with the following formula:

$$\frac{\text{GRAMS OF FAT PER SERVING} \times 9}{\text{TOTAL CALORIES PER SERVING}} = \frac{\text{PERCENT OF CALORIES FROM FAT}}{}$$

$$\left(\text{Example:} \quad \frac{8 \times 9}{310} = \frac{72}{310} = 22\%\right)$$

INDEX

A

B

C

MW = Microwave Directions, MWO = Microwave Directions Only

MW = Microwave Directions, MWO = Microwave Directions Only

Pictured left to right: Bean and Bacon Combo p. 14, Hearty Grain Quick Loaf p. 42

MW = Microwave Directions, MWO = Microwave Directions Only

**Pictured left to right: Valentine Rolled Cookies
p. 78, Chocolate Cherry Surprise Cookies p. 78**

MW = Microwave Directions, MWO = Microwave Directions Only